The Nurturing Father's Program

Developing Attitudes and Skills for Male Nurturance

Facilitator Manual

by Mark Perlman, MA

Center for Growth & Development, Inc. Publishing
3277-D Fruitville Road, Suite 1
Sarasota, Florida 34237
Toll Free 1-888-390-1119

The Nurturing Father's Program
Developing Attitudes and Skills for Male Nurturance
Facilitator Manual

by Mark Perlman, MA

Copyright © 1998 by Mark Perlman, MA
Published by Center for Growth & Development, Inc. Publishing

The **Nurturing Father's Facilitator Manual** describes the activities for *The Nurturing Father's Program.* It is designed to be utilized with A Nurturing Father's Journal/Workbook and other program materials. For additional information on the Nurturing Father's Program, contact:

Center for Growth & Development, Inc.
3277-D Fruitville Road, Suite 1, Sarasota, Florida 34237

Toll Free 1-888-390-1119
Fax: 941-953-9552
E-mail: mcperl@verizon.net
www.nurturingfathers.com

ISBN# 0-9662927-1-5

Printed and bound in the United States of America.

10   9   8   7   6   5   4   3   2   1

Dedication

To Barney, my father,
and nurturing male role model,

To my wonderful sons,
Jaime and Corey,
with whom I have learned and grown;

and to all the men dedicated
to being nurturing fathers.

Acknowledgments

To **Kate McPhillips,** my wife and partner, for her love, support, wisdom and dedication;

Stephen Bavolek, father of the ***Nurturing Programs for Parents and Children,*** nurturing ambassador, and mentor;

Vicki Rollo, book design and illustration;

John Marcus, editor, consultant (and pizza lover);

Lisa Paulson, word processing and computer assistance;

Alan Glassberg, Jim Burns, Vinny Boyle, for field testing the program and helping to shape the final outcome;

Phyllis Perlman (thanks for everything, Mom);

Alan Perlman, music and brotherhood;

Trout, for the use of his relevant and insightful cartoon;

Janet Perlman (co-parent), Jared and Alice Massanari, Marc Weinberg, Joe Ferrandino, Fran Kaplan, Paul Burns, Alice Taylor, Judy Ruf, Margo Burchim-Glassberg, Peter Howard, Ishmael Katz, Bill and Carol McPhillips, valued friends, colleagues, and extended family;

The Monday Night Men's Group; and the **Father's United Network (FUN of Sarasota, Florida).**

"The reality is that 'parent' is still usually taken as a code word for 'mother'. When 'parenting groups' are advertised, they are usually understood as invitations to women and when parenting research is done, it is usually heavily based towards mothers. The only way to find out what is happening for the 'invisible parent' in America was to point the spotlight directly and specifically at him. Nurturing isn't just something fathers do, but something that men do."

– James Levine, Director
The Fatherhood Project
Fatherhood USA
Kilnman, D. and Kohl, R., 1984

"The supreme test of any civilization is whether or not it can teach men to become good fathers."

– Margaret Mead

The Nurturing Father's Program

Table of Contents

List of Posters

Symbol Key

 Refer to or complete assignment in the *Nurturing Father's Journal*

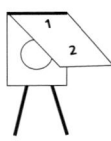 Use flip chart/blackboard

 Refer to specific poster

 Split up into small groups

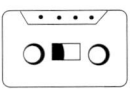 Use audio tape

Introduction

Nurturing Father

A man who actively provides guidance, love, and support to enhance the development and growth of children for whom he cares.

You are about to embark on an adventure - one that will take you into the hearts, minds, and lives of men who want to care for their children and families in a nurturing way. This adventure may lead you through hopes and fears, laughter and tears, as well as memorable relationships and experiences. You will deepen your knowledge of the men with whom you share this journey, and hopefully deepen your knowledge of yourself along the way.

This *Facilitators Manual* will be your trusted companion for this adventure. Serving as your road map and guide, it will enable you to lead your group through safe and valuable experiences that contain the potential for new learning and growth. These introductory sections will help you use the manual so that you successfully reach the final destination: helping men discover and cultivate their nurturing potential.

I hope you enjoy this adventure as much as I have.

The Nurturing Father's Program: Overview

Rationale:

Children need their fathers.
Fathers need their children.
Throughout history fathers have been considered a valuable and important part of both a child's and a family's life. Recent research overwhelmingly supports the benefits that accrue to children and families through positive father involvement.

This research also strongly points out the unique benefits that men gain through active involvement in fathering and family life. Nurturing fathering enhances the growth and well-being of men as well as children (and women who are part of the family unit).

For a family to experience these benefits, however, fathers must be present. Father absence not only denies these benefits, but it is shown to be harmful to child development and well-being. The presence of the father is only the beginning, however. It is the *quality* of his presence that matters most in enhancing the life of his children and other family members. The nurturing father brings those attitudes, values, and skills to children and family that best support growth, development, and stability.

Recent history gives serious cause for concern about the roles fathers are playing in the lives of children and families. Many adult men and women associate the traditional father with the role of the cold, detached disciplinarian – a far cry from the nurturing father. And, today, too many children awaken each morning with no father in their home (and often, in their lives). The number of children living apart from their biological father has more than doubled, from 17% in 1960 to 36% in 1990. And if this trend, the product of the dramatic increase in divorce and out-of-wedlock births, continues, more than 50% will live apart from their fathers by the year 2000. Seventy percent of white children and ninety-four percent of black children will live apart from one of their parents before they reach the age of 18. (And in 86% of single-parent families, the custodial parent is the mother.)

The results of fatherlessness are tragic for both children and families. Juvenile crime has increased six-fold since 1960, and evidence points to the absence of the father as a major factor in the increase of delinquency and violence.

60% of rapists
72% of adolescent murderers > **come from fatherless homes**
70% of long-term inmates

38% of America's poor are children, and 73% of children in single-parent families will spend some time in poverty. Child abuse rates have risen, and evidence shows that a strong bond between a father and child in the early years (first three years) may be a critical factor in preventing later abuse.*

Some current thinking suggests that perhaps the father's role is a dispensable one, that it is unnecessary for rearing healthy children. The above statistics and overwhelming evidence point to the contrary. The father plays a valuable, unique and irreplaceable role.

In parenting and family life, two adults ease the many demands and stresses that accompany child-rearing and managing a family. The very differences between the two parents can also provide a broader base for solving problems and stimulating growth and development in children.

Besides the traditional role of fathers being both provider and protector (this role is still of great value and can be shared with a spouse or partner), there are contributions that only a father can make and that the nurturing father provides in a very positive way. Fathers teach little boys how to be men. Fathers teach daughters how to relate to men, and feel deserving of respect and love. Fathers have a unique style of playing with their children, which teaches self-control and helps them modulate their behavior. Fathers stimulate risk-taking and independence. They promote respect for rules and discipline. The presence of the father increases empathy and well-being. (Children whose father spent time alone with them more than twice a week tested higher in empathy and became more compassionate as adults. The researchers who conducted this 26-year longitudinal study termed this finding "quite astonishing.")*

The undeniable conclusion from the large amount of available research and evidence as well as from what so many of us know in our hearts to be true is that CHILDREN AND FAMILIES GREATLY BENEFIT FROM THE PRESENCE AND PARTICIPATION OF A NURTURING FATHER.

And we as fathers know the incomparable joy, growth, and sense of well-being that is available to us through our children and family relationships.

The Nurturing Father's Program was created to cultivate and support the attitudes and skills for male nurturance, hoping to benefit men, women, and children in family relationships.

* (The data cited above is from *Life Without Father*, David Popenoe, Martin Kesler Books/The Free Press, New York, 1996.)

A Male Group Experience

Fathering is the male parenting role, and it is learned primarily from the male/father/father-figures in our lives. While we also learn much from the female/mother/mother-figures in our lives, including lessons about parenting and nurturing, fathering is the male parenting practice.
I recommend it be taught by men and for men. It is my belief and experience that the most powerful group process for learning nurturing fathering is men working with men – sharing histories, hopes and fears, and thoughts and feelings that arise from the male experience. The intimacy and support available in this group setting is unique and powerful. Many men/fathers have never had such intimacy or support from other men, including their own father. The all-male group format allows for a re-fathering experience, in which men support and nurture one another's growth and development as nurturing fathers.

This is not meant to imply any disrespect for the mother/female role. I hold it in the highest esteem, so much so, that I would suggest the same all-women format for a mothers program, if its focus would be the mothering role. Groups composed of women and mothers, etc., have had a significant place in our culture for some time, and I have drawn inspiration from that model in suggesting this all-male group experience to facilitate nurturing fathers.

With that said, I must add that this is only a suggested format derived from my experiences. If people using this program choose to include women as facilitators or participants, I would be interested in hearing about the experience and learning from it.

Method: How Parenting Is Learned *

The following describes the foundation on which *The Nurturing Father's Program* was developed. It is important for facilitators to understand this learning model because it explains how this program is structured in order to facilitate learning and growth, as well as achieve its objectives.

We tend to parent the way we were parented. In other words, we learn parenting from our parents (or the parent role-models in our life). Since parenting is a learned behavior, it can be relearned. Change and new learning are possible. With exposure to new experiences, parenting attitudes and practices can be influenced and changed. The diagram on the following page illustrates how parenting is learned (or relearned).

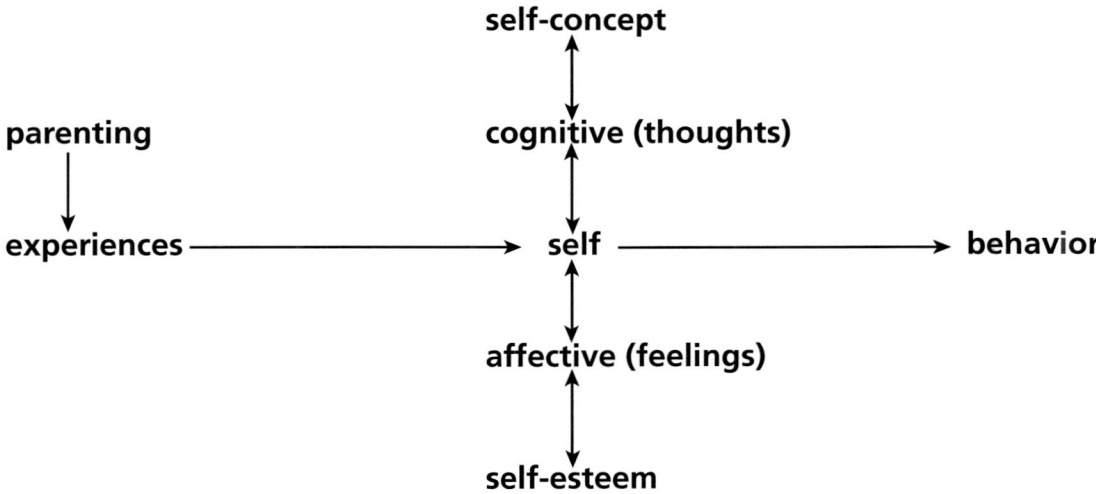

Parenting (or how we were parented) leads to experiences that directly impact us in two ways:

1. **Cognitively** – messages that lead to thoughts that develop into self-concept or "what we think about ourselves."

2. **Affectively** – feelings that develop into self-esteem or "how we feel about ourselves."

Our self records these experiences as self-concept and self-esteem.

It is our self-concept and self-esteem that lead to behavior. Our parenting (behaviors and attitudes) can be traced back to our self-concept and self-esteem.

The Nurturing Father's Program is structured to provide fathers with *experiences* that allow the self new cognitive (thinking) and affective (feeling) responses, thus providing the *opportunity* to change parenting attitudes and behaviors. As a result, program participants can choose to reshape and relearn fathering, to let go of old fathering practices that do not bring desired results and to adopt new nurturing ones that achieve the established goals. The growth in self-concept and self-esteem can lead to more nurturing, rewarding relationships with children, spouses/co-parents, and other family members. Therefore, *The Nurturing Father's Program* is created on an experiential learning model, which provides activities that stimulate thinking and feeling in a supportive group atmosphere.

* (Adapted from *Teaching Nurturing Parenting Skills*, Stephen Bavolek, Ph.D., 1991.)

Program Design and Practical Considerations:

The *Facilitators Manual* contains the complete program design and instructions for the 13- weekly group sessions. Each session contains specific objectives that represent the learning goals for that week. These objectives are formulated into activities, which lead group members to experiences from which they can learn and grow.

Room and Seating: A moderately large room is desirable so that up to 20 men can be seated in a large circle of chairs.

Group Size: It is recommended that the group consist of from 12 to 16 men, plus one or two facilitators. Plan for some members (up to three or four) to choose not to continue after Week 1, so begin with a few more members than you need for the desired group size.

Note: For Week 8, **"Playshop,"** a larger room may be needed in order to accommodate the children and activity areas. The facilitator may suggest a different location (perhaps outdoors) and/or time (perhaps a weekend) if this suits the group members.

For Week 13, **"Graduation,"** the room must be large enough to accommodate children, spouses/co-parents, or other family members.

Time: Each weekly meeting will be two-and-a-half hours long. The facilitator should be sure that meetings begin and end on time. Not only is this considerate, but it establishes the group norm that this time is to be valued and respected. Request that members call the facilitator if they will be absent or late. The facilitator should inform the group when a member cannot attend.

Snack & Social Time: About halfway through each session, there will be a 15-minute break for snacks and social time. This should be a fun and nurturing time for the group to socialize and get to know one another better. It is suggested that the facilitator bring the snacks and drinks for Week 1. Then ask one group member each week to bring the snacks for the following meeting. This will give the men the opportunity to "host" one week and nurture the group.

Home Activities: Each weekly meeting will end with Home Activities to be done during that week in the *Nurturing Father's Journal.* The facilitator must emphasize the importance of doing the Home Activities if members want to gain the maximum benefits from the program. A great deal of learning and growth will take place outside the group sessions. In fact, many sessions will begin with a review and discussion of the Home Activities from the previous week.

Group Hug: A large circle group hug is the closing activity for each meeting. It is very important to end with this ritual. Although hugging may be difficult or uncomfortable for some men at first, it will create tangible benefits for the group. Encourage members to actively participate while respecting individual comfort levels. The group hug becomes easier with practice, and it often produces valuable interactions.

Materials: In addition to the materials contained in the Nurturing Father's Program, the facilitator should have the following items on hand: a flip chart; markers; pencils or pens; name tags; masking tape. An audio tape player is needed for certain weeks. As the facilitator reads the weekly activities in preparation for the group, note the specific materials required for that week.

The posters included with the program will serve as useful teaching tools and will save time and effort for the facilitator. Again, as you review the instructions for each week's activities, note which posters are to be used.

Confidentiality: The program contains a confidentiality agreement. The importance of confidentiality will be discussed in Week 1 along with the ground rules for the group. Each group member and the facilitator will sign the confidentiality agreement, which the facilitator will collect and keep for the duration of the program.

Certificates: A Certificate of Achievement is awarded to each group member who completes the Nurturing Father's Program. Attending at least 10 of the 13 sessions is suggested as a guideline for program completion. The facilitator may exercise flexibility and personal judgment for deciding which members are to receive certificates. Completion of the activities in the **Nurturing Father's Journal** is an important factor to consider.

Program Evaluation: A special program evaluation form is provided for each member to complete in Week 12 and to return to the facilitator. This will provide the group members with the opportunity to share their thoughts and feelings about their experiences in the program and to make suggestions for improvements. The evaluation will also provide useful feedback for the facilitator. The information generated from the evaluation will assist in planning future programs and can be used to promote the program as well as appeal to funders for financial support.

The attitudes and skills contained in the 13-week **Nurturing Father's Program** represent many of the foundational blocks upon which nurturing fathering is built. Yet they are only part of the total parenting picture. As children and families grow, needs and relationships change, and with this fathers and fathering must also change and grow. Continuing education, essential for all important jobs, is highly recommended for fathers, spouses/co-parents and children. Other good parenting programs are available to enhance and build upon what was learned in *The Nurturing Father's Program.* I recommend the *Nurturing Programs for Parents and Children* as an ideal next step. These programs are based upon the same principles as *The Nurturing Father's Program* and they include participation of all family members (adult and children). They offer the best choices of age and issue-specific parenting.

Facilitator Role and Guidelines

Facilitate means "to make easy." The key role of the facilitator is to make the group learning experience easy for the members. This involves creating a safe, comfortable and encouraging space for men to be open and to explore. Qualities such as honesty, openness, respect, good communication, humor, and humility go a long way in creating a positive group process.

Although it would be helpful for the facilitator to have had experience as a father/mentor/role model and truly value and enjoy this role, it is not necessary to be a fathering or parenting expert. None of us knows "all the answers," but if we stay focused on the program materials, share our own experiences, and encourage other members to contribute, valuable learning will occur. The facilitator should refer to the program content and use the collective experience of the group when addressing specific problems or issues brought up by members. There is a delicate balance in leaving time for individual problems and areas of concern or interest, while maintaining focus and ensuring adequate time each session for all of the program activities. The program is designed so that individual and group experience builds and develops from week to week, creating a total experience that incorporates all of the program's learning objectives. Have faith in the process!

The following guidelines may be helpful for successful group facilitation:

One person can successfully facilitate the program. Co-facilitation is enjoyable, and it may be desirable when it is practical. Two facilitators add a depth and richness of experience, and they can better attend to individual and group needs. If you co-facilitate, be sure to meet weekly to prepare for each session, to divide the primary responsibility for different activities and to share perceptions.

It would be helpful if the facilitator has had some experience running groups, teaching parenting education, or has had experience in a counseling role.

Share your personal experience and invite group members to do the same.

Do not judge or criticize. Instead, refer back to the program content for suggested practices and tools.

Some problems will be beyond the scope and time of this program. Be knowledgeable about resources in your community so that you can make appropriate referrals. Know the reporting laws of your community regarding child abuse, domestic violence, and other issues pertaining to safety and protection.

Allow for silence and non-participation. It takes some individuals and some groups more time to relax and become involved in the process. Encourage participation and feel free to experiment with creative approaches to it.

Humor and laughter are to be encouraged, as they can enhance the group process. Humor in all male groups seems to be natural, and it builds trust and camraderie.

Do not pressure yourself to be "perfect." We all make mistakes or sometimes simply "don't know." Openly acknowledging your mistakes will win the trust of the members. This will also serve as a model that will encourage the members to be more open and vulnerable, and this is extremely relevant to nurturing fathering.

Enjoy, and know that by facilitating this group experience, you will be making a significant contribution to the group members, their children and family members, and to your community.

So . . . thank you!

Notes:

Week 1

The Roots of Fathering

Program Objectives - Week 1

To introduce group members to The Nurturing Father's Program.

To share introductions by group members.

To clarify the relationship between our father's (or father figure's) and our own style of fathering.

---

15 min.   Welcome! Program Introduction

Express a warm welcome to the men in the group. Let them know that you're glad that they are here and acknowledge the courage and commitment it takes to be in the group. Hand out the **Nurturing Father's Journal** to each group member and state the importance of doing the home activities in the journal each week. Ask members to turn to **page ix**. Tell them a little about **The Nurturing Father's Program,** highlighting the following points:

Program length: 13 weeks

Each weekly meeting lasts two and a half hours

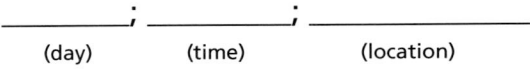
_____; _____; _____
    (day)   (time)   (location)

There will be one break, about halfway through the meeting, with snacks and social time (we suggest that each week a different member bring the snacks).

Time in the group will be ACTIVE, with the members participating in and experiencing different activities that stimulate thoughts and feelings.

Each week the activities will focus on specific attitudes and skills that are related to nurturing fathering. We will learn together by experiencing these attitudes and skills and by discussing the nurturing fathering process. This will be a _safe_, supportive place in which to learn and explore.

Each week there will be home activities to do, using the **Nurturing Father's Journal** as a guide. These activities are extremely important to the success of the program.

15 min.   Group Member Introductions

Facilitator should participate in these personal introductions. Introduce yourself first to "model" this one-minute personal introduction.

To begin the process of getting to know one another, ask each group member to present a one-minute introduction about himself. (Note: Introduction about his role as a father will come later.)

Write on flip chart/blackboard:

"My name is _____."

"A few things I'd like you to know about me are _____."

"What I hope to get from this program is _____."

45 min.   Fathering His-Story

Refer each member to **page 3 of *A Nurturing Father's Journal*** in order to complete **"Fathering His-Story."** Allow a few minutes for the group members to prepare their his-story, and ask them to take three minutes to present their fathering introductions.

A) I am the father/stepfather/grandfather/male guardian of:

_____

(name and ages of children)

B) My immediate family includes:

_____

(spouse, co-parent, others)

C) Brief history as a father:
   – Becoming a father (circumstances surrounding the choice or situation)
   – Birth(s) (your experience around the birth[s])
   – Transitions (your experience with divorce, death, or other family change)

Monitor the time and remind members of the three-minute time frame for making their presentations. After all members have spoken, ask the group if anyone has a comment or perception they want to share.

15 min.   Break & Snacks

---

10 min.   Ground Rules

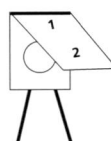

Explain that every group needs basic guidelines in order for the members to work together and accomplish the goals. Write the following ground rules on the flip chart/blackboard and discuss each one:

– Begin and end on time.

– Confidentiality. Hand out the confidentiality agreement to all group members. Each member reads and signs the agreement, which is a statement of respect for one another as well as a promise to maintain confidentiality.

– Communication. One person speaks at a time. Listen to one another respectfully, without any interruptions.

– Accept differences of opinion. These differences can be the seeds for growth and learning.

– Actively support one another. We are on a path together as nurturing fathers.

– Bring your full self here: your thoughts, feelings, and experiences. Respect what each member shares.

– Ask group members if they have any other ground rules to suggest.

15 min.   Visualization: My Father and Me, Part 1

Explain that the following activity gives each member the opportunity to explore the important connection between himself and his father (or primary father figure in his life).

Important Note:
Those group members who did not know their father or whose father was absent should focus on the meaning of that father-absence. This will be important for some members.

Directions:
Use enclosed audio tape (Side A) for a narrative presentation of this visualization or read aloud using audio tape (Side B) for musical background to accompany your reading.

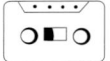

"Sit comfortably in a relaxed position with your eyes closed and take a few deep breaths. Let any tensions go. Relax as you breathe normally and travel back in time.

Return to your boyhood (any age), to a place where you and your father would be together. Notice the surroundings. Notice the details of the place. How do you feel being there?

Now your father enters. What do you feel? Notice these feelings. (pause) How does your father look? (physical size, body type, clothing, face, anything else that comes to mind.) (pause)

What kind of father was he? (pause) List the qualities that fit him. (pause)

Take a closer look.

How do you feel in his presence? (pause)

How did he discipline you? (pause)

What did he do when he was angry at you? (pause)

How did he relate to your mother? (pause)

How did he teach you or explain things to you? (pause)

Were you afraid of your father? (pause)

How did he show love? (pause)

Did you play together? (pause)

How did you and your father have fun? (pause)

Do you notice anything else about this man who was a father to you? (pause)

Is there anything you want to say to him before you leave? (pause)

Father fades from the picture. Take a deep breath as you let him go.

With another deep breath, notice your body being supported by the chair. Slowly open your eyes and rejoin us here."

---

30 min.   My Father and Me, Part 2

 Direct group members to page 5 of *A Nurturing Father's Journal.*

Ask each member to write all the words, qualities, and phrases that describe his father or primary father figure, and to do this without any talking. For those members whose father was absent or unknown, ask them to describe what the absence left them with and anything they heard from others about their father.

Explain the primary connection between the father that we are in relation to who our father was. We learn how to be a father from our father or father figure. We tend to father the way we were fathered. A powerful link exists between us and our father. This fact should be acknowledged and respected. But we are not condemned to repeat our father's mistakes.

 Direct members to form small groups, with three members in each one. Provide the following directions for a small-group discussion:

Each group member takes five minutes to introduce his father (or father figure) by describing the qualities and information that were identified in the visualization exercise. Be sure to include how you felt as a child about these characteristics of your father and his fathering style.

(Monitor the time and remind group members to limit their presentation to five minutes each.)

After all members have presented, allow for a large group discussion about feelings, common themes, and whatever else the experience brought up.

JOURNAL

Ask members to refer to the cartoon "Boxes" (below and on page 6, *A Nurturing Father's Journal).*

"It's a bunch of stuff my dad gave me. I'm going to go through it and save some, throw some away, and add some of my own."

Facilitator: Discuss how a conscious acknowledgment of who our father was and how we felt about him as a child allows us (as adult men and fathers) to make choices about our own fathering style.

Discuss the cartoon.

5 min.   Home Activities

> Remind group members of the importance of doing the home activities each week. The activities will deepen and strengthen their nurturing attitudes and skills as well as create a personal record for them to keep and reflect back on.

Ask group members to:

> Complete the "Vision Statement: The Father I Choose To Be" *(page 7, A Nurturing Fathers Journal).*

> Bring a memento of your father (a photo, object, story, song, letter, etc.), anything that represents something significant about him to you.

> Consider your ethnic/cultural background (e.g., African-American, Hispanic, Jewish, Irish, Japanese, Chinese, Hawaiian, American Indian, others) and the role of the father in your culture. Complete "Fathers Come in Different Cultural Styles" *(page 9, A Nurturing Father's Journal).*

End with a group hug.

All group members stand shoulder to shoulder and form a circle with their arms around one another.

Let group members know that each meeting will end this way.

Note: The group hug may be difficult for some men who are uncomfortable being that close to other men. Encourage the experience, yet accept the boundaries and comfort needs of each member. An alternative is for the member to stand shoulder to shoulder without his arms around other members. The comfort level should increase as the weeks progress.

Thank members for their participation and contributions to the group and encourage them to return the following week.

Week 2

Self-Nurturing Skills I: Fathering "The Little Boy Within"

Program Objectives - Week 2

To share visions of "The Father I Choose To Be."

To explore different cultural styles of fathering.

To learn to identify the "little boy" within each man/father.

To learn to establish a nurturing relationship (self-nurturing) with this little boy.

---

5 min.   Welcome

Let returning members know how glad you are to see them. If new members have joined, conduct very brief introductions, then ask the new members to review the ground rules from Week 1 as well as sign the Confidentiality Agreement. (Both of these can be done during the break, but it is important to commit to them verbally.)

---

40 min.   Home Activities Review

Ask each group member to read or explain the personal information generated from "Vision Worksheet: The Father I Choose to Be" *(page 7, A Nurturing Father's Journal)*. Suggest that each member express this information without discussion or comment from the other members, the goal being to encourage an atmosphere of attentive and respectful listening.

After all the returning members have presented their vision statements, ask if the new members would like to make a statement about the father they choose to be.

Following the completion of all vision statements, suggest that the members frequently read and reflect on their vision during the following weeks.

25 min. **Fathers Come in Different Cultural Styles**

In this section the group will focus on the role of the father in different ethnic/cultural groups. Ask members to refer to "Fathers Come In Different Cultural Styles" *(page 9, A Nurturing Father's Journal).* Using this as a reference, ask one group member to identify his ethnic/cultural group, then to describe the role of the father in that group. Next, ask all members of that same ethnic/cultural group to contribute to the description of that style of fathering. Then, ask members from another ethnic/cultural group to describe their culture's fathering style. (Note: Not all members of a culture may agree; allow for different experiences and descriptions.) Continue this process until all ethnicities/cultures represented in your program have shared some of their norms and styles related to fathering.

Note that these ethnic/cultural influences should be considered as each member chooses what to "keep" or "throw away" for his personal fathering style.

15 min. **Break & Snacks**

20 min. **Mementos of Our Fathers**

Ask each group member to share a memento of his father (photo, object, story, song, letter, etc.) and explain what it represents about his father and/or their relationship. Try to draw out a feeling from each member about the memento and his father.

Questions to help draw out feelings:

– *How do you feel about that?*

– *What does that mean to you?*

– *How has that affected you?*

– *Does anyone have a feeling about what _____ just expressed?*

(name)

If some members did not bring a memento, ask them, "What is the main feeling that you have toward your father?" Accept all answers and keep the activity moving along.

---

10 min.

Our Unmet Needs from Childhood - "The Little Boy Within"

Use the following information to help the group members understand the concept of "the little boy within." Explain the idea and give examples, then ask the group for examples to ensure that they understand the concept.

- We have been discussing our father and his relationship (or lack of relationship) with us.

- We were the child/the little boy growing up.

- As a child, none of us got all our needs met from our father or mother. Each of us has unmet needs - some more than others.

- For example, if our father was absent, we may have needed more of his time and attention. If our father hit or yelled a lot, we may have needed kindness or protection. If our father criticized us, we would have liked to have heard "good job" or "great effort." Perhaps we needed to hear "I love you."

- Ask the members for other examples of unmet needs from childhood.

- These unmet needs are often still in us today, as if that little boy is still asking to be cared for and to have his needs met. The little boy that we were still lives within us and deserves to have his needs met.

- But our fathers are not here to meet these needs.

- We, as adults, can notice these unmet needs (the little boy within) and respond in a nurturing manner. Each of us can be a nurturing father to ourselves, to the unmet needs of the little boy within.

- This will help us and make it easier to be a nurturing father to our children.

5 min.   Visualization: "Fathering the Little Boy Within"

Directions: Use enclosed audio tape (Side A) for a narrative presentation of this visualization or read aloud using audio tape (Side B) for musical background to accompany your reading.

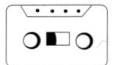

Guide the group in the following visualization:

"We will now take a few minutes to get to know the little boy within us. Close your eyes and imagine a little boy inside of you. He is you when you were a child growing up. Picture this little boy. (pause)

Ask what he is feeling. (pause)

Do or say something that will comfort him. (pause)

Ask the little boy what he needs, and listen carefully to his answer. (pause)

Reassure this little boy that you care about what he needs and want to meet his needs. (pause)

Say good-bye and give the little boy a hug."

After a short pause, ask members to take a deep breath, then open their eyes to rejoin the group.

20 min.   "Fathering the Little Boy Within, " Part 2

Direct members to remain silent and to form small groups (three or four members in each one). Once the groups have been formed, instruct each member to describe the experience of the little boy.

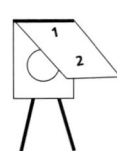

Write the following questions on a flip chart or blackboard to help each member focus on important information:

– "What did you notice about this little boy?"

– "What feelings did he have?"

– "What needs did he have?"

– "How do you normally respond to such feelings and needs?"

– "Do you respond like your father responded to you?"

– "How can you better respond as a nurturing father?"

Remind the groups to leave time for each member.

---

5 min.   **"Fathering the Little Boy Within," Part 3**

Call the large group back together and discuss what was learned through the activity. Summarize the small group discussion and note any common themes. Most importantly, no matter where members are with the experience, encourage each man to recognize and nurture the little boy within.

---

5 min.   **Home Activities**

➤ Complete the worksheet entitled "My Little Boy Within" *(page 15, A Nurturing Father's Journal)*

➤ Reread "The Father I Choose to Be" vision statement from Week 1. Practice being this father to your little boy within. This begins an awareness of self-nurturing, which we shall focus on the following week.

End with a group hug.

Week 3

Self-Nurturing Skills II: The Power To Meet My Own Needs

Program Objectives - Week 3

To identify principles and practices for meeting one's own needs.

To identify strategies for overcoming blocks to self-nurturance.

To formulate encouraging messages for meeting specific needs.

---

15 min.   **Home Activities Review**

What more did you learn this week about your little boy within?

What was your experience (positive or negative) in practicing being a nurturing father to your little boy within?

---

15 min.   **Self-Nurturing Principles**

Ask members to turn to page 21 of *A Nurturing Father's Journal* and discuss the following:

(Write each of these principles on a flip chart or use enclosed poster and allow a brief discussion on each one.)

– All human beings (men, women, and children) have needs.

– Some needs must be met in order to stay alive.
  (Ask for examples.)

– Some needs simply feel good when they are met.
  (Ask for examples.)

– Who is primarily responsible for meeting your needs?
  I am primarily responsible for meeting my needs.

– My ability to meet my needs is Personal Power.

– Meeting my needs in a positive way is self-nurturing.
  (Ask for examples.)

– Can I meet my needs in a negative way? Yes, and this is self-destructive. (Ask for examples.)   I have a choice.

– My ability to meet my needs in a positive way (self-nurturing) helps me meet the needs of (nurture) others, e.g., my children and spouse/partner.

---

60 min. Self-Nurturing Practices

Explain that the group will now focus on practical ways to identify and meet individual needs, and achieve balance in six important need areas.

Direct group members to form six small groups (two to three members in each one). Ask one member to serve as the recorder for each group.

Have six sheets of flip-chart paper with one of the following words written across the top of each one: PHYSICAL, SOCIAL, EMOTIONAL, INTELLECTUAL, CREATIVE, SPIRITUAL.

Give one piece of paper and a marker to each group. Then direct the members to think of every positive way that they can to meet the needs in that particular area, and to write them down on the piece of flip-chart paper (allow 10 minutes), e.g., positive ways to meet physical, emotional or spiritual needs.

When each group has finished, give each one a second sheet of flip-chart paper and ask the members to write the ways in which they BLOCK themselves from meeting these needs. Blocks are the specific ways in which we deny, avoid, or distance ourselves from meeting our needs, e.g., overwork, ignore physical symptoms, escape through food, TV, alcohol, etc.

For each block, write strategies to overcome that block. (Allow 15 minutes for this exercise.)

As each small group completes its work, tape the flip chart papers around the room so the entire group can see them.

Gather everyone back together and ask a representative from each group to present:

A) The ways to meet the needs in their specific need area.

B) Suggestions for overcoming BLOCKS. (Allow 35 minutes total, approximately five minutes for each group presentation.)

Remind members to pay special attention to any need area in their lives that is empty or lacking. The goal is BALANCE in filling all six need areas.

15 min.   Break & Snacks

10 min.   Self-talk: Discouraging and Encouraging Messages, Part 1

Explain that self-talk describes the statements we silently make to ourselves, inside our head. Some of these statements are left over messages from childhood. Some of these messages are self-nurturing and encourage us to meet our needs. Others are discouraging and block us from meeting our needs. We can use our self-talk to create encouraging messages that motivate us to meet our needs.

Then explain that in the following activity they will identify:

Discouraging messages: identify any discouraging messages (possibly from childhood) e.g., "I don't deserve to be happy," "I'll never be popular," "It is selfish to meet my own needs."

Encouraging messages: members should change the discouraging message to a positive, encouraging one, e.g., "I deserve to be happy," "I can be well-liked and popular," and "It's okay to meet my own needs."

15 min. Self-talk: Discouraging and Encouraging Messages, Part 2

Direct members to turn to page 24 **in *A Nurturing Father's Journal*** and to complete the activity entitled "Self-talk: Discouraging and Encouraging Messages."

This activity involves listening to our self-talk and changing discouraging messages to encouraging messages.

Discouraging Messages ⎯⎯$\xrightarrow{\text{to}}$⎯⎯ Encouraging Message

Explain that group members should feel free to add any additional encouraging messages that they feel will help them to meet their needs in a positive way.

Be available to assist any group member who may be struggling with this activity. It will be helpful to enter into a dialog with that person to enable him to identify discouraging messages and to create encouraging ones.

10 min. Self-talk: Discouraging and Encouraging Messages, Part 3

Ask members to break into small groups, with four to six members in each one. Direct each member to state to his group one of his encouraging messages, in a style that shows he truly believes it. Next, wait and have him emphatically repeat the message. Then move to the next member. Repeat this process until all members have stated and repeated an encouraging message. Continue going around the circle until each member has stated all of his encouraging messages.

Explain that the purpose of each member stating and repeating each encouraging message is to practice and reinforce the skill of using positive self-talk.

5 min.   Self-talk: Discouraging and Encouraging Messages, Part 4

Call the groups together and ask the members how they feel
after this activity. Encourage all members to continue sending
encouraging messages to themselves, even if it feels difficult.
Self-nurturing is like a muscle that strengthens with use.
Encouraging self-talk strengthens our capacity to nurture.
It can feel like hard work at first, but it pays off.

5 min.   Home Activities

➤ Complete "A Plan for Meeting My Own Needs" *(page 22-23,*
  A Nurturing Father's Journal).

➤ Review "Self-talk: Discouraging and Encouraging Messages,"
  and practice saying encouraging messages to yourself this week.

End with a group hug.

Week 4

The World of Feelings and Male Nurturance

Program Objectives - Week 4

To accept feelings as a normal aspect of human experience and to reflect on our ability to experience and express a wide range of feelings.

To identify guidelines for relating to other people's feelings in a nurturing way.

To define the nurturing characteristics that are shared by both fathers/males and mothers/females.

To identify the nurturing characteristics that exemplify the father/male style of parenting.

---

15 min.   Home Activities Review

Ask group members to share their self-nurturing experiences from the previous week. (Accept all experiences, whether they were successful or not.) Then ask members to summarize the details from "A Plan for Meeting My Own Needs," again encouraging attempts at self-nurturing. Encourage the group to provide support and suggest additional strategies where appropriate. Then remind members that they need to be patient with themselves, that any new skill takes time and practice in order to be developed.

Becoming good at self-nurturing will take time. It is important to forgive any mistakes that are made because they represent learning opportunities. Group members must practice patience, encourage one another, and give praise for their efforts. Always celebrate a success.

Monitor how many group members are relating to their little boy within and if they are using self-nurturing messages.

45 min.   Relating to Feelings

Our Own Feelings
Inform group members that they will spend some time focusing on feelings, first on their own, then on others'. Ask the members to complete the worksheet "Relating to My Feelings" *(page 29, A Nurturing Father's Journal).* This should take five to seven minutes. Point out that two questions will be asked about each feeling. The first will regard feeling or experiencing a feeling, and the second will pertain to expressing the feeling. For example: "I felt sad (experienced sadness) when I learned of my father's death" and "I cried when I heard that my father was dead." Or, "I felt excited when my team scored" and "I cheered and jumped when my team scored."

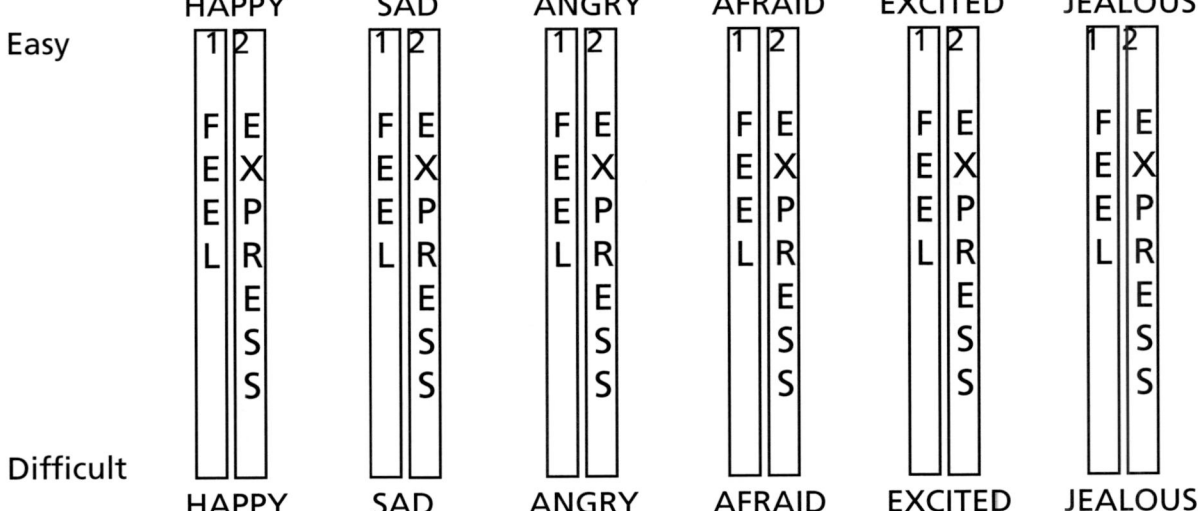

After all the members have completed the worksheet, poll the group to chart their responses to each feeling, both how they feel it and how they express it. Note each individual's response on the flip chart graphic by placing a dot on the bar between "Easy" and "Difficult." This will indicate the group's general response to feeling and expressing the feelings on the chart.

Initiate a discussion about men and their feelings, using the questions listed below and help the group draw conclusions.

Some feelings may be easy or difficult to feel/experience. Why?

Some feelings may be easy or difficult to express. Why?

Do you think men and women differ in how they experience and express feelings?

Which feelings are easier for men to experience or express? (Anger is often easier.)

Can the group think of others?

Which feelings are more difficult to experience or express? (Sadness, fear, and jealousy often fall into this category. Why?)

Men are taught as young boys to view these feelings as "weak" because they make them feel vulnerable and out of control. Women are taught just the opposite, that these feelings are okay, but they are often taught that anger isn't permissible.

Both men and women, boys and girls, have the capacity to feel and express the full range of feelings. It is part of being human. In fact, feelings connect us to experiences and people. As a result, feelings are part of intimacy: being connected to other people, being in touch with them.

By men/fathers learning to feel and express the full range of feelings appropriately, they can experience greater intimacy with their children, spouse, etc. And in so doing, they will model and teach their sons and daughters how to feel and express their own feelings.

Agree to use this program to practice experiencing and expressing the full range of feelings.

Note: This can certainly be overdone. Feeling too much or expressing feelings too much (as with anger) will be addressed in Week 6.

20 min.   Relating to Others' Feelings

As men/fathers in intimate relationships – with children, a spouse, or a partner – we often witness other people's feelings. Sometimes these feelings can be very intense. The following are guidelines for nurturing ways of responding to them.

Note: The focus here is on others' feelings, not troublesome behaviors. Such behaviors will be addressed later in the program.

List the following on a flip chart/blackboard or use enclosed poster and discuss each one.

– Feelings are deep and personal, and they are important expressions of one's self. Do not deny another person's feelings. Accept them and acknowledge them.

– Identify a feeling by its name, e.g., "Oh, you seem to be sad" or "Are you afraid ?"

– Help the other person express the feeling (in ways that won't hurt self or others). Let the person talk. Let them display the feeling safely, e.g., cry for sadness, jump up and down with happiness, shout into a pillow for anger, etc.

– Be there for another person and their feelings. This is part of nurturing fathering.

15 min.   Break & Snacks

15 min.   Male Nurturance, Part 1

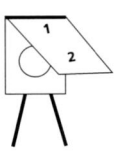

Ask the group members to name as many nurturing qualities or characteristics that they can. Chart the responses on a flip-chart/ blackboard (without any discussion). Be sure to include all nurturing characteristics that parents can express to children of any age.

Ask group members to identify which of these nurturing characteristics are common to both fathers/males and mothers/females. Then discuss ways in which they are shared by both groups. Some examples might be expressing love and encouragement, non-sexual touching, role modeling, and setting limits. Have members add to the list other nurturing qualities common to mothers and fathers.

---

30 min.   Male Nurturance, Part 2

Ask group members what might be the differences in the male and female style of nurturing/parenting. Note these differences on the flip chart/blackboard under the headings "Male Nurturance" and "Female Nurturance." Allow for discussion, including some possible disagreement. Accept any differing points of view. Avoid the "nature vs. nurture" argument, i.e., whether these differences are genetic or learned.

Example: Regarding styles of play, research has observed differences in the types of interactions between young children and their fathers and mothers. Fathers tend to be physical and play "rough," while mothers tend to hold and comfort, using toys to mediate play.

Ask members to be open and to consider the possibility that fathers practice a different style of nurturing/parenting in certain ways.

There is no right or wrong way. All nurturing parenting practices are acceptable, and they play a role in a child's growth and development.

Summarize the list of possible differences between male and female nurturing as follows:

Male/Father	Female/Mother
• Focus is on doing, emphasizing performance and competence	• Focus is on being, emphasizing acceptance and safety
• Risk taking	• Protectiveness
• Boundaries/rules/standards	• Emotional attunement, empathy
• Teaching independence	• Teaching relatedness
• Justice/fairness	• Forgiveness
• Role model for male/father	• Role model for female/mother

Allow additional characteristics for discussion.

Understand that these qualities or styles are not mutually exclusive. They do not belong to the domain of the father or mother. We are all capable of each one, and we can practice all of them, and should probably be encouraged to do so.

Indeed, fathers and mothers should cultivate the nurturing qualities that are common to both, as discussed earlier. And we as fathers should embrace and honor the nurturing qualities that we feel pertain more to men.

---

10 min.   Home Activities

➤ Complete "My Feelings" *(page 30, A Nurturing Father's Journal)*.

➤ Instruct the group members to complete "Fathering Practices," *(page 34, A Nurturing Father's Journal)*. Members should note in the left-hand column the fathering practices that they consider to be nurturing, e.g., hugs, compliments, praise, family rules, etc. They should indicate in the right-hand column the practices that they feel are non-nurturing, e.g., hitting and yelling. Ask the members to list fathering practices regardless of whether they actually use them. This is important information, and it will be discussed at the next meeting.

End with a group hug.

Reminder: Even if the group is running late, never leave without the group hug. This activity is central to facilitating nurturing fathering.

Notes:

Week 5

The Power To Nurture: Fathering without Violence or Fear

Program Objectives - Week 5

To differentiate between nurturing and
non-nurturing fathering practices.

To identify the intentions and actual outcomes
of various fathering practices.

To commit to the use of specific nurturing
fathering practices that do not represent
fear or violence.

To understand the differences between "power-
over" and "power-to" and how they affect
men's lives.

---

60 min.   Home Activities Review

Ask group members to share the nurturing and non-nurturing
"Fathering Practices" from their list in ***A Nurturing Father's
Journal*, page 34.** Then generate a composite list on the flip
chart, emphasizing what makes each fathering practice nurturing or non-nurturing. Avoid judging the practices as good or
bad, right or wrong. Instead, focus on outcomes, what results
from them. Utilizing the chart on the following pages, describe
common fathering practices in terms of the "intended goal"
and "actual outcome."

See intended goals/actual outcomes table on pp. 32-33 of this
manual. Refer members to ***pages 40-41, A Nurturing Father's
Journal.*** Two important questions to ask when evaluating a
fathering practice:

1. *How's it working?*

2. *What will be the results or outcomes?*

15 min. Fathering without Fear or Violence, Part 1

Present the following analysis of the fathering practices in terms of male power and the use of fear and violence.

State that all the nurturing fathering practices have a few very important things in common: THEY ACCOMPLISH THEIR GOALS WITHOUT USING FEAR OR VIOLENCE.

Ask each group member to take a minute and go within himself and consider these questions: "Do I want my children to fear me?" (pause) "Do I want fear and violence to be in the fabric of my relationships with those whom I love?" WE HAVE THE POWER TO CHOOSE.

Display enclosed poster for Week 5 (Discipline from "disciple". . .) and refer to it during the following discussion.

State that all the non-nurturing fathering practices use fear and violence. Allow for discussion, if needed.

Explain that the choice each group member makes now will play a major role in determining

    A) what his child will become as s/he grows up

    B) the nature of the relationship between him and his child.

Explain that fathering through fear and violence leads to blind obedience and/or rebellion, while fathering that utilizes the nurturing practices without fear or violence leads to respect, cooperation, and self-responsibility.

Discipline from "disciple". . .
It's about leading and teaching.

Intended Goals and Actual Outcomes

Fathering Practices	Intended Goal (parent)
Hitting (corporal punishment)	Getting their attention. Stopping undesired behavior. Teaching discipline. Teaching respect.
Yelling	Getting their attention. Communicating something of importance. Teaching discipline and respect.
Put-Downs (criticism)	Attention to undesired behavior. Stopping undesired behavior. Teaching "what not to do."
Expressing Love	Instilling feelings of love and well-being.
Encouraging	Facilitating growth and development. Facilitating competence and performance.
Praise	Attention to desired behavior. Teaching "what to do." Showing parental approval.
Hugs	Non-sexual physical expression of love, tenderness.
Giving Choices	Empowerment. Learning to analyze and solve problems.
Consequences	Teaching discipline and responsibility. Discouraging undesirable behavior.
Listening	Learning about child's thoughts and feelings. Communicating interest and caring.
Family Rules	Setting limits. Balancing adult and child needs and desires. Learning what is not okay vs. okay

Actual Outcome (child)
Gets their attention. They see anger/violence. Hurts physically and emotionally. Damages self-esteem. Teaches violence/power-over. Leads to revenge, fear.
Child turns off and shuts down, does not hear message. Hears anger, violence, power-over. Feels badly about self (lowers self-esteem). Leads to revenge, fear, disrespect.
Child feels hurt (lowers self -esteem). Undesired behavior gets attention. Doesn't teach "what to do." Leads to discouragement, withdrawal, resentment.
Feels love and lovable. Increases self-esteem, sense of well-being and ability to express love to others.
Promotes will to succeed, to take risks, to grow, to learn. Ability to tolerate failure.
Increased self-esteem and self-concept. Tendency to repeat desired behavior. Sense of well-being, love, encouragement.
Feels loved, secure, safe. Increased self-esteem.
Feels empowered (power-to). Learns to analyze and solve problems. Leads to self-responsibility.
Learns self-discipline and self-responsibility.
Increased self-esteem. Sense of personal value and worth. Feels cared about and motivated to communicate with parent.
Learns limits and self-discipline. Practices respect and self-control. Learns social skills.

Challenge

Can I lead without FEAR and VIOLENCE? The choices (and outcomes) are mine!

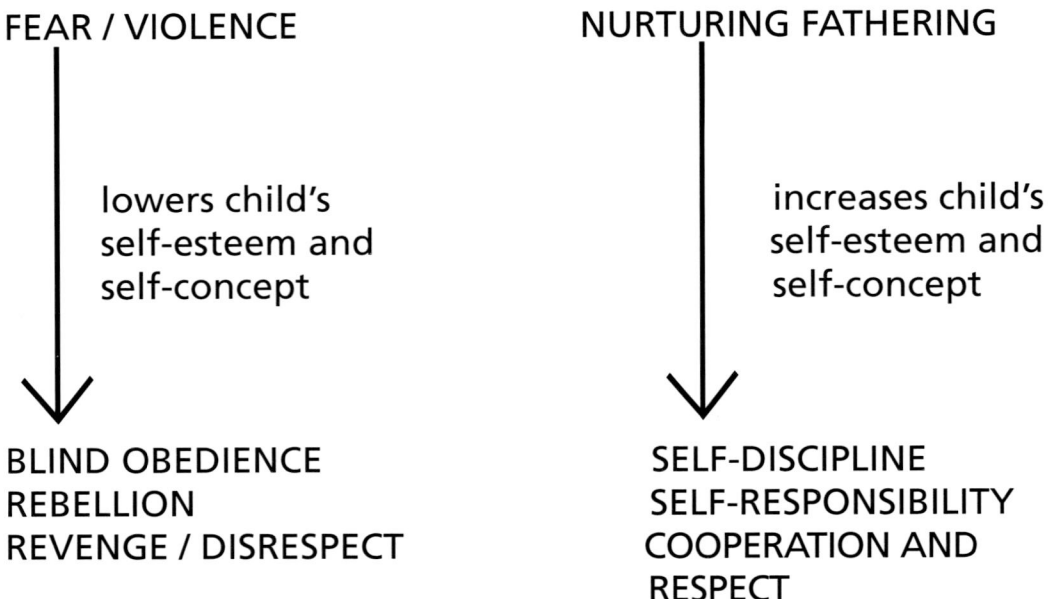

FEAR / VIOLENCE	NURTURING FATHERING
lowers child's self-esteem and self-concept	increases child's self-esteem and self-concept
↓	↓
BLIND OBEDIENCE REBELLION REVENGE / DISRESPECT	SELF-DISCIPLINE SELF-RESPONSIBILITY COOPERATION AND RESPECT

NOTE: Respect is something you must give in order to receive.

The shepherd guides his sheep with the staff (leading without violence).

15 min.   Break & Snacks

---

10 min.   Fathering without Fear or Violence, Part 2

Ask group members to return to their list of fathering practices, *(page 34, A Nurturing Father's Journal)* and circle the practices they choose to use and cross out the ones they choose not to use.

20 min. **Fathering without Fear or Violence, Part 3**

Instruct group members to divide into small groups, three to four members in each one. Ask each member to share his list of chosen fathering practices (from the above) with the discussion focusing on:

– reason for the choices

– anticipated challenges or difficulties

– help or support desired from the group

(Remind the groups of the time that has elapsed so that all members will have a turn.)

---

25 min. **Styles of Power: "power-over" and "power-to"**

Use the enclosed poster or copy "power-over"/"power-to" diagram (page 36) on a flip chart.

Begin this section with the following introduction:

All people want and deserve to be empowered, to feel powerful. But different "styles" of using power yield different results. One style can bring harm to others and to relationships, while another can be helpful to others and to relationships.

The change from a "power-over" style to a "power-to" style is a central, pivotal concept in this program. If you choose to let it happen, it can be transformational to you as a nurturing father.

It can transform your relationship to yourself (your physical body, emotions), your children, your spouse, even to the world.

Let's look more closely at the transformative potential of this simple notion.

Ask the members to refer to the "power-over"/"power-to" diagram. Review each section (from left to right) and encourage comments, questions, and discussion.

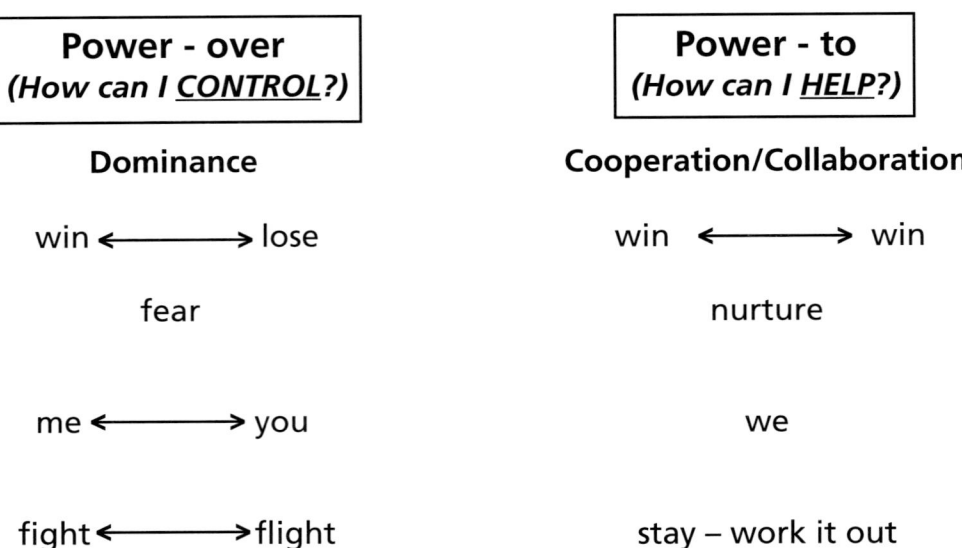

Power - over *(How can I __CONTROL__?)*	Power - to *(How can I __HELP__?)*
Dominance	**Cooperation/Collaboration**
win ←——→ lose	win ←——→ win
fear	nurture
me ←——→ you	we
fight ←——→ flight	stay – work it out

Here is an analysis of the "power-over"/"power-to" diagram to assist you in explaining the diagram:

In the "power-over" style: The central question a man asks is "How can I control . . . the situation, the child, my spouse?" etc. He is most comfortable dominating others, making them sub-servient and less powerful. He sees conflict in terms of winning, with the other/opposition losing. He uses fear to preserve his dominance and control. This creates distance between himself and other people – me vs. you. In challenging and tense situa-tions, he will either fight (to win) or take flight (leave) to avoid losing, e.g., leave his children during a difficult divorce.

In the "power-to" style: The central question this man asks is "How can I help . . . the situation, the child, my spouse?" etc. He often helps through joining with others in collaborative and cooperative efforts. He shares his power with others, and helps others use their power constructively. He learns to see conflict as an opportunity for creative problem solving where everyone can "win" (get some of their needs met).He recognizes that nobody likes to "lose." He leads through nurturing, and others feel drawn to him. This ease and close-ness create a "we" rela-tionship, instead of a "me vs. you." In challenging and tense situations, he will stay and find ways to work things out (resolve conflict, solve problems), e.g., find ways to continue to be a nurturing father during a difficult divorce.

Most men are a unique mix of these two styles of power, perhaps closer to one or the other. The nurturing attitudes and skills taught in this program encourage movement toward the "power-to" style.

Next, using the chart on the following page entitled "Changing Power-over to Power-to" discuss the key areas and how group members can be affected by this change. Refer members to **page 45 in *A Nurturing Father's Journal.***

The change from a "power-over" style (which focuses on controlling, dominating, and winning) to a "power-to" style (focusing on helping, enhancing, and cooperating) is central to this program. It is imperative that group members understand the positive results that this concept produces and how transformational it can be. While the concept itself is fairly simple, applying it can be challenging and requires time, patience, commitment, and support. As facilitator, reinforce this concept whenever possible, especially when it has created a success. Use the group process to help confront obstacles and barriers in an effort to encourage adopting this new behavior.

Changing "Power-over" to "Power-to" and How It Affects Men's Lives

	POWER-OVER results in...	POWER-TO results in...
The Little Boy Within	Denying his existence, controlling his expressions. Cannot acknowledge needs and ask for help.	Being open to his needs, messages, and longings. Can identify and provide for own needs and is able to ask others for help.
Physical Body	Blocking its subtle messages; becoming inflexible, out-of-touch. Denying needs and warning signs.	Being in touch with the body's rhythm and messages, able to respond and address the physical needs and warning signs.
Emotions	Controlling the "vulnerable" emotions (fear, sadness). Not feeling or expressing them. Anger as the primary vehicle for emotional release. Limited intimacy.	Feeling and understanding one's deeper emotional selves and sharing this with others. Anger balanced with other emotions, and expressed in non-destructive ways. Greater capacity for intimacy.
Children	Control, dominance, fear, distance, leading to rebellion. (This can result in physical abuse, rape, or sexual abuse.)	Respect and admiration, leading to relaxed relatedness, role modeling, intimacy, empathy.
Spouse/Co-Parent/ Intimate Others	Power struggle, conflict, one-way communication, leading to fear, tension, attacking problems through win/lose. Distance from other people.	Cooperation, compromise, two-way communication, leading to relaxed relatedness, real teamwork, creative compromise and problem solving, intimacy. Closeness to other people.
Leadership	Control, dominance, isolation, "my way = right way," motivated by personal ego needs ("I"). Results in low productivity, low morale, low creativity and initiative.	Visionary, mission/goal-driven, collaboration and teamwork, mediates conflicts. Utilizes differences creatively. Motivated by benefit to the common good ("We"). Results in higher productivity, high morale, high creativity and initiative.

5 min. **Home Activities**

➤ Read "Power-over vs. Power-to" *(page 44, 45 & 46, A Nurturing Father's Journal).*

➤ Read page 42 and complete "My Nurturing Fathering Practices" *(page 43, A Nurturing Father's Journal)* and put them into practice this week.

➤ Complete "Unconditional Love" *(page 47, A Nurturing Father's Journal).*

➤ Be patient with yourself and your child/ren. This is a learning process. Bring successes and failures to group next week. We learn from both!

End with a group hug.

Notes:

Week 6

Overcoming Barriers to Nurturing Fathering

Program Objectives - Week 6

To recognize anger, alcohol/other substances, and stress as potential barriers to nurturing fathering.

To analyze the dynamics of anger and identify tools to manage it.

To understand the relationship between excessive anger and alcohol/other substances and to increase the awareness of group members' patterns of alcohol/substance use.

To practice stress-reduction techniques.

---

25 min. Home Activities Review

Ask group members how things are going for them at this point in the program. Also ask them to summarize "My Nurturing Fathering Practices" *(page 43, A Nurturing Father's Journal)* and to describe their successes or struggles over the past week in applying them. Provide and encourage praise and support for all efforts. Help the group to problem-solve any difficulties/failures and encourage continued practice of the nurturing fathering techniques.

Using the above discussion, identify potential barriers to nurturing fathering, highlighting excess anger, alcohol or other substance abuse, and also stress. This week will focus on developing an increased understanding of and ability to manage these potential obstacles.

45 min.   Managing Anger - Understanding the Dynamics of Anger and the Tools for Managing It

Explain that anger is a natural, normal human emotion. Ask the group, "When does anger become a problem?" and accept all answers. Explain that anger is not a problem in itself, but what we do with our anger is the problem. If we hurt others with our anger, it is surely a problem and also a barrier to nurturing fathering. Ask for examples of this, such as hitting, yelling, throwing things, etc. Anger is a powerful feeling, and it can feel out of control. But that does not mean that we are powerless over the feeling, that it can make us do things that we later regret.

Draw the following diagram on the flip chart:

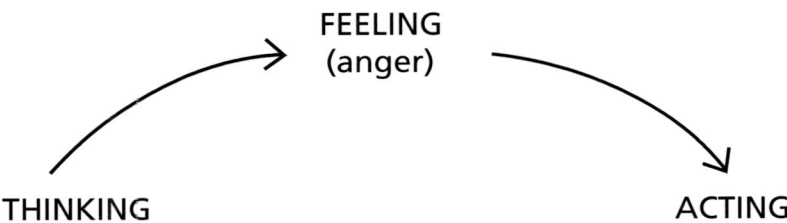

FEELING
(anger)

THINKING   ACTING

Explain that if we look closely at our anger, we can see that something precedes it and that something also follows it.

Anger is preceded by THINKING. In fact, certain thoughts are the fuel that fires up anger, and the more we throw these thoughts on the fire, the hotter the feeling of anger becomes. Discuss this by using the following example:

Our two-and-a-half-year-old child screeches "no" and throws his toy on the ground. Ask group members what thoughts can fuel anger in this situation, e.g.: "My son is being defiant," "My daughter doesn't respect me," "My son will grow up with no discipline."

The first thing to do in order to manage anger is to take a step back and look at the thoughts that precede the emotion, then change the thinking:

inaccurate	to	➜	accurate thoughts
negative	to	➜	positive thoughts
non-nurturing	to	➜	nurturing thoughts

Ask the group to look at the thoughts from the above example, then to change them to reflect a more accurate, nurturing vision of the two-and-a-half-year-old's behavior, e.g., "Kids that age say no a lot," "Independent but a little too strong," "Angry but not a good way to express it by throwing things."

Note: This entire thinking process caused the father to STOP, PAUSE, and REFLECT. This is positive in itself.

What follows the THINKING ➜ FEELING is ACTING, taking action and doing something. We can choose an action that is not violent or destructive. The pausing and reflecting that was done in the above situation should make the next step easier. In any case, what we do with our anger and the energy that accompanies it is within our control. (In fact, by using this process, we maintain control over ourselves and therefore the situation at hand, as opposed to acting out of control.)

If stopping, pausing, and reflecting has decreased the anger, then you can deal directly with the child's behavior by using a nurturing fathering practice, e.g., giving choices and explaining the consequences. For example, "If you throw your toys, we'll have to put them away for a while. But if you can play without throwing them, then we'll leave them out."

If the feeling of anger is still strong and can lead to violent action, then something must be done (action) with this energy (anger).

Ask for suggestions from the group for dealing with the anger/ energy. Possibilities include: walking away from the situation; asking your spouse/partner to take over; taking a run around the block; writing down the angry thoughts and feelings; yelling into a pillow (being careful not to scare the child/ren);

calling a friend or a group member you've learned to trust; attacking the problem (not the person) by trying to figure out what you can do to change the situation; evaluating the consequences of taking different actions. Mention that fathers can help their children deal with their own anger by showing them how to use these same techniques.

Note: If you notice a group member struggling with excessive anger, speak with the person in private and supportively recommend counseling or group therapy, or an anger-management program.

15 min.   Break & Snacks

10 min.   The "Families and Chemical-Use Questionnaire," Part 1

Introduce the questionnaire **(page 56, A Nurturing Father's Journal).**

Explain that the word chemical is being used to refer to any mood-altering substance, including alcohol, illegal drugs, and even some prescription drugs. Ask group members to take 10 minutes to complete the form, emphasizing the need for honesty with their answers. State that the questionnaire is for their own information about their patterns and/or problems and that details need not necessarily be shared with the members of the group. What they learn, however, can be discussed with others in order to get support as well as establish plans for removing obstacles to nurturing fathering.

10 min.   The "Families and Chemical-Use Questionnaire," Part 2

Direct members to form small groups, three to four members in each one. Suggest that each group discuss the conclusions and insights gained from completing the questionnaire. Also, ask the groups to problem-solve and lend support to any member who feels that chemical use may be an obstacle for him to nurturing fathering.

Note: If you recognize that a group member is struggling with an alcohol or substance-abuse problem, arrange a private discussion in which you recommend obtaining counseling, attending AA meetings, or getting some other appropriate type of treatment.

10 min.   The "Families and Chemical-Use Questionnaire," Part 3

Gather all members together and facilitate a discussion on the problems of alcohol and other mind-altering substances. The following questions and accompanying information can guide the discussion:

- "What is the relationship between alcohol (or other substances) and anger?" *Alcohol decreases inhibitions and can release stored-up anger. Judgment becomes impaired, and the anger can result in others being hurt.*

- "What is the relationship between alcohol and auto fatalities?" *Alcohol is a factor in at least 50% of all traffic deaths each year.*

- "What do children learn when they observe their father drunk or using illegal substances?" *They learn that it's okay to get drunk or break the law.*

- "How can excessive use of alcohol or drugs harm families? *It leads to secrecy. It teaches victimization. It creates family dysfunction, which children replicate when they become parents. It can also create serious personality disorders in children.*

Important Guidelines:

- Do not use illegal drugs.

- If you drink alcohol, drink in moderation.
  (moderation = no more than one or two drinks in a 24-hour period)

(Taken from *Nutrition and Your Health: Dietary Guidelines for Americans,* Third Edition, 1990, U.S. Department of Agriculture, U.S. Department of Health and Human Services.)

10 min.   Reducing Stress, Part 1

A simple explanation of stress is that it's our instinctual animal response to real or imagined danger. The body and emotions prepare us for a protective response (fight or flight). This is healthy and normal. We then return to rest. Modern life, however, is full of stressors, for example, work demands, financial concerns, traffic jams, divorce, etc., and these can lead to long-term, chronic stress. This can impair one's health, emotional well-being, and relationships.

Chronic stress often indicates an imbalance in one's life, and this imbalance requires an adjustment. The adjustment can be practical/situational (e.g., cutting back on work, using time management, problem solving, changing habits or routines, etc.) or attitudinal/self-talk (e.g., expect less from ourself, alter goals, be less self-critical and more positive, etc.).

Summarize the above information for the group, then ask how chronic stress can affect fathering. Generally, it presents an obstacle to nurturing fathering by leaving little time, energy, and/or patience for children and family.

10 min.   Reducing Stress, Part 2

Ask the group to describe what helps them to manage stress and restore balance to their life. Use the enclosed poster to discuss the "Guidelines For Stress Management."

Guidelines For Stress Management

– Take time for yourself to meet your needs (refer to Week 3, "A Plan For Meeting My Own Needs").

– Prioritize essential tasks. Let non-essentials wait.

– Exercise regularly.

– Eat well.

– Listen to your body (do not deny the body's messages, such as pain and discomfort).

– Play. Laugh. Kids can help us do this. (The next two weeks of the program will focus on these areas.)

– Utilize problem solving. (See Week 10, "Teamwork between Father and Spouse")

– Practice relaxation exercises.

---

10 min.   **Reducing Stress, Relaxation Practices, Part 3**

Directions: Use enclosed audio tape (Side A) for a narrative presentation of this visualization or read aloud using audio tape (Side B) for musical background to accompany your reading.

Ask group members to get in a comfortable position, either sitting or lying down. Guide them in three relaxation exercises: breathing, muscle release, and visualization.

Read the following: "Get in a comfortable position, either sitting or lying down with your body relaxed and fully supported. Close your eyes and pay attention to your breathing. Inhale slowly and deeply, then exhale. (pause)

As you breath in, feel the clean energy filling your body. As you exhale, let go of any tension or stress. Relax. (pause)

Now, breathing normally, tighten the muscles in your feet and legs. Hold for a few seconds and release. Now, tighten your stomach, pelvic, and buttock muscles. Hold. Release. Now make a fist, squeeze and tighten your hands, your arms, your shoulders. Hold, then let go. All tension flows away. Now tighten your face and scalp, your eyes, nose, and mouth, then release. Your body is fully relaxed, free of any pain and tension. (pause)

Picture in your mind a peaceful place, one that you know well, where you feel perfectly at ease. It may be a lake or river, the woods, a mountain top, or a private place all your own. See it clearly, and feel the pleasure of being there. (pause for a minute or two)

Remember, this place is always there for you, and you can take a 'brief vacation' in your mind whenever you choose to, at any point during your day.

Take another slow, deep breath as you feel the vital life force fill your body. Then exhale. One more deep breath, then release.

Now, breathing normally, feel your body and the surface around you. Slowly open your eyes, as we return to the room."

---

5 min.   Home Activities

➤ Complete "Father Play: Fun & Games," *(page 58, A Nurturing Father's Journal.*

➤ Ask group members to review all the journal material they have done so far and to note progress made in any areas.

End with a group hug.

Notes to Facilitator:

Weeks 1, 2 and 3, dealing with the roots of one's personal fathering experience and developing self-nurturing skills, can have a positive impact regarding anger management and stress reduction.

Week 9, which concerns active listening and reflecting, and Week 10, which addresses negotiation and conflict resolution, offer additional tools for helping to reduce anger and conflict.

Unexpressed or repressed hurt can lead to excess anger. As fathers uncover or identify past or present hurts and learn to express them more openly and appropriately, anger should begin to decrease.

Be cognizant of any problems with anger management, alcohol and/or substance abuse, and excessive stress. This program is not group therapy, and it does not treat these conditions. Please recommend appropriate treatment in your local community for group members who could benefit from it.

Be aware of child abuse and neglect reporting laws in your community, and let group members know that you must follow these laws if children could be endangered.

Week 7

Discipline and Fun & Games

Program Objectives - Week 7

To learn the key to techniques for discipline and
behavior management through an
understanding of team sports.

To establish family rules for the whole family.

To establish guidelines for nurturing play and
plan a Playshop for our children.

---

15 min.　　Discipline and Team Sports, Part 1

How "the game" is played

Introduce this section by informing group members that we will
be using our understanding of team sports to learn some important tools for disciplining children.

Begin with the following points:

Most of you know something (perhaps a lot) about team sports,
e.g., basketball, baseball, football, hockey, soccer, etc.

You may have played (or still do), watch, or have some familiar-
ity with how a team sport is played.

If you understand how team sports work, you probably know
more than you think you do about disciplining children.

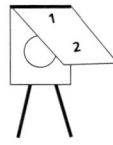 Let's take the sport of basketball, for example. (You can use any
of the aforementioned sports). Draw the basic court on a flip
chart/blackboard.

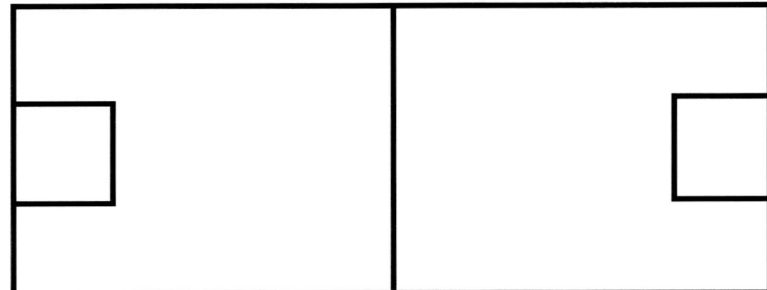

In order to start playing, what does everybody have to know and understand about the game?

The goal: to get the ball into the basket

The lines and the rules: what they mean

What to do to win

The penalties (consequences) for breaking the rules

It is also important to remember:

To work together - teamwork

What one member does (good or bad) affects the whole team

Encourage the "good"

Discourage the "bad"

---

60 min.   Discipline and Team Sports, Part 2

Discipline = teaching children to play by the rules so that they can be part of the team (family, school, society, etc.).

Let's take a closer look at how this analogy between team sports and discipline works.

FIRST, THE GOALS. Set up the playing field in a way that helps the child and family succeed (win). For example, if you have a toddler, move all fragile or valuable objects out of the child's reach because toddlers explore and get into things. Put child-proof locks on cabinets where dangerous chemicals are stored. This is called "baby proofing" your home. It will also help you say "no" less frequently to the child.

An example for a teenager would be to remove all alcoholic drinks from your home or keep them in a locked cabinet in order to discourage teenage drinking. Set up the game with the goals in mind.

Understand and explain the "game." For a family, the goals are to work together, to be safe and happy, to learn and to grow, and to help each member get their needs met, without denying others. What one member does affects everyone (the whole team). Discipline is helping the child play by the rules so s/he will achieve the above goals.

SECOND, THE RULES. The rules must be clear and everyone must understand them. If there are no rules, or if the rules are not explained clearly, you cannot expect children to learn to play the game. (Note: It will be helpful if the children participate in creating the rules. This will give them more ownership and respect for the rules. As children get to be pre-teens and teens, this becomes essential.)

Ask members to return to the team-sports diagram and explain the rules of the game. What do the lines represent? What other rules are essential to the game? Point out that rules really have two parts:

Rules have two parts: Do's (what to do) and
Don'ts (what not to do).

EXAMPLES:

Do's (What To Do)	Don'ts (What Not To Do)
Play within the lines	Don't step outside the lines
Play hard/be safe	No hitting or hurting
Speak in a calm voice	No yelling or cursing

Also, note that:

The rules apply to *everyone.* Therefore, you and your child/ren (and spouse) will create family rules, e.g., "no hitting" applies to all family members; so does putting things away after using them.

An explanation as to why the rule is important is helpful. Remember, rules have a "WHAT TO DO" for every "WHAT NOT TO DO."

THIRD, ENCOURAGE TEAMWORK AND DESIRED BEHAVIOR.
Ask group members what team players do every time a player
makes a foul shot, makes a good pass (assist) or scores a goal/
touchdown, etc. They give the person a pat on the back, high-
five, verbal compliment, etc. Every time!

There must be some special value in encouragement. What you
pay attention to you are likely to see more of. Encourage,
praise, and reward the behaviors that you want to see more of,
the "what to do" list.

Ask group members for effective methods of encouragement,
praise, and reward. Be sure to include:

– Praise - "well done," "good job," etc.

– Encouragement - "great effort," "good try," "thanks for . . ."

– Positive Touch - hug, pat on the back, high-five, etc.

– Expanded Privileges - more time to play, more mature
  activities, more of what the child values/desires, etc.

– Rewards - objects, money.

– Pay attention to the positive. This will have a powerful effect on
  shaping and encouraging the desired behavior (playing by the rules).

FOURTH, DISCOURAGE MISBEHAVIOR. Establish clear consequences for breaking the rules. If the consequences can be
logically related to the transgression, then the child will learn
more from the consequences. When a rule is broken, begin with
a warning/reminder. State the "what not to do" and the "what
to do."

The warning/reminder is stated as a choice followed by a consequence. It would sound something like this:

"If you stop yelling (what to do), then you can keep playing the
game. But if you continue yelling (what not to do), then you'll
take a five-minute time-out. It's your choice." Such choices and
consequences teach discipline, and self-responsible behavior.
There is an undesirable penalty/consequence for misbehavior.

If the misbehavior occurs again, follow through with the consequence. Consistency is very important. (Note: Anger and violence are not part of the game. The referee never uses anger or violence to enforce the rules in team sports.)

Examples of CONSEQUENCES for discouraging misbehavior:

TIME-OUT (sit on the sidelines). "If you can't play by the rules, then you'll have to sit out for a while." The time-out should be brief, two to ten minutes, depending on age.

BEING GROUNDED (big infraction; you miss a game). "If you get into a fight at school (what not to do), then you will stay home after school and won't play with your friends. If you do not get into any fights (what to do), then you can go out and play."

LOSS OF PRIVILEGE (can't be on the starting team). "If you do not put your toys away when you're finished playing (what not to do), then you cannot play with them after your nap. But if you put them away (what to do), you can play with them later."

RESTITUTION (fines, payback). Pay for or replace what was lost or broken. Provide a service for breaking the rules. "If you take your sister's music tape without asking (what not to do), then you'll have to let her keep one of your tapes. Or, ask her if you can borrow a tape (what to do), then it's no problem."

That's the game plan. The family is a team, with parent(s) as both coach and referee. *Discipline is helping your child/ren to become a team player and to learn to play by the rules.*

15 min.   **Break & Snacks**

15 min.   **Father Play: Fun & Games, Part 1**

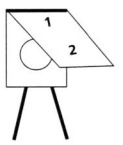

Ask members to provide specific examples of fun games and activities (referencing "Fun and Games" *page 58, A Nurturing Father's Journal)* that they recall from their childhood or currently enjoy with their children. These should be listed on a blackboard or flip chart. For each fun game or activity, members should indicate the elements that were present (or absent) that made the activity fun.

10 min.   Father Play: Fun & Games, Part 2

Review the enclosed poster entitled "Guidelines for Nurturing Play" *(page 69, A Nurturing Father's Journal)* with group members. Using examples from the previous activity, help members relate these guidelines to their examples.

"Guidelines for Nurturing Play"

– Nobody gets physically hurt. Safety comes first.

– No one gets emotionally hurt. Avoid criticism and put-downs.

– Everyone is encouraged to participate.

– Reward effort, not perfection. (Build self-esteem and confidence.)

– Minimize teaching and instruction.

– Lead with encouragement and modeling.

– It's okay to give and receive help.

– Encourage teamwork and cooperation.

– The goal is to have fun.

– Dads, let your "little boy within" out to play.

Note: Make any adjustments that are needed because of the child's age, physical size, or skill level. If the child and game don't fit, change the game.

30 min.   Father Play: Creating a Playshop

Instruct the group that it will now create and plan a Playshop for the next meeting. Their children (from ages 3-17) will also be invited to attend.

Note: Facilitator can be flexible on the ages of the children and time and location of the Playshop, depending on the make-up of the group. For example, if fathers have mostly very young children, shorten the format to one hour, or hold the Playshop at a day care center, or during the day on a weekend. Poll the group members to determine the number and ages of children who will attend the Playshop.

Using the guidelines and the list of fun games and activities generated earlier, a two-hour experience will be created for fathers and children to play and have fun together. Four groups will be assembled for planning the playshop activities.

Suggested Playshop Format:

1 Hour	Welcome and introductions. Four play stations are set up, each with a different fun game or activity. Children, assembled in four groups, spend 15 minutes at each activity/play station. (Older teens can serve as helpers to assist smaller children.)
15 min.	Fun Snacks - all together
15 min.	Songs - all together
30 min.	Stories, either read or told - all together
End:	Group hug - all together

Direct members to break into four groups. Each group will: (1) choose one fun game/activity to be set up in a corner of the meeting room and ensure that the necessary materials/props are available; (2) choose a simple, fun song that everyone can learn and sing together; (3) choose a story to tell, read, or create together (be sure all the children's ages and skill levels are planned for); (4) finally, choose a special snack or drink to bring.

Periodically inform each group of how much time is left so that the planning for activity/game, snacks, songs, and stories will be completed.

After all four groups have completed their planning, ask each group to state what fun game or activity it will host at its play area. Logistical details should be worked out as needed. Groups should also explain what snacks, songs, and stories will comprise the Playshop.

Note: Researchers have observed that many fathers engage in physical play to challenge, stimulate, and arouse their child. This impacts the child's learning and skill development. This type of father-child interaction can influence a child's ability to manage frustration, explore new activities, and solve problems in a creative way.

5 min.   Home Activities

➤ Read the section entitled "Discipline and Team Sports" *(page 63-66, A Nurturing Father's Journal).*

➤ Set aside time this week with all family members to discuss and complete "Family Rules" *(page 67, A Nurturing Father's Journal).*

➤ Make careful plans for the Playshop with the group members in advance so that all the materials that will be needed will be on hand. The emphasis will then be on having fun.

Suggestion: Bring name tags for fathers and children.

End with a group hug.

Notes:

Week 8

Playshop: Fun & Games for Fathers and Their Children

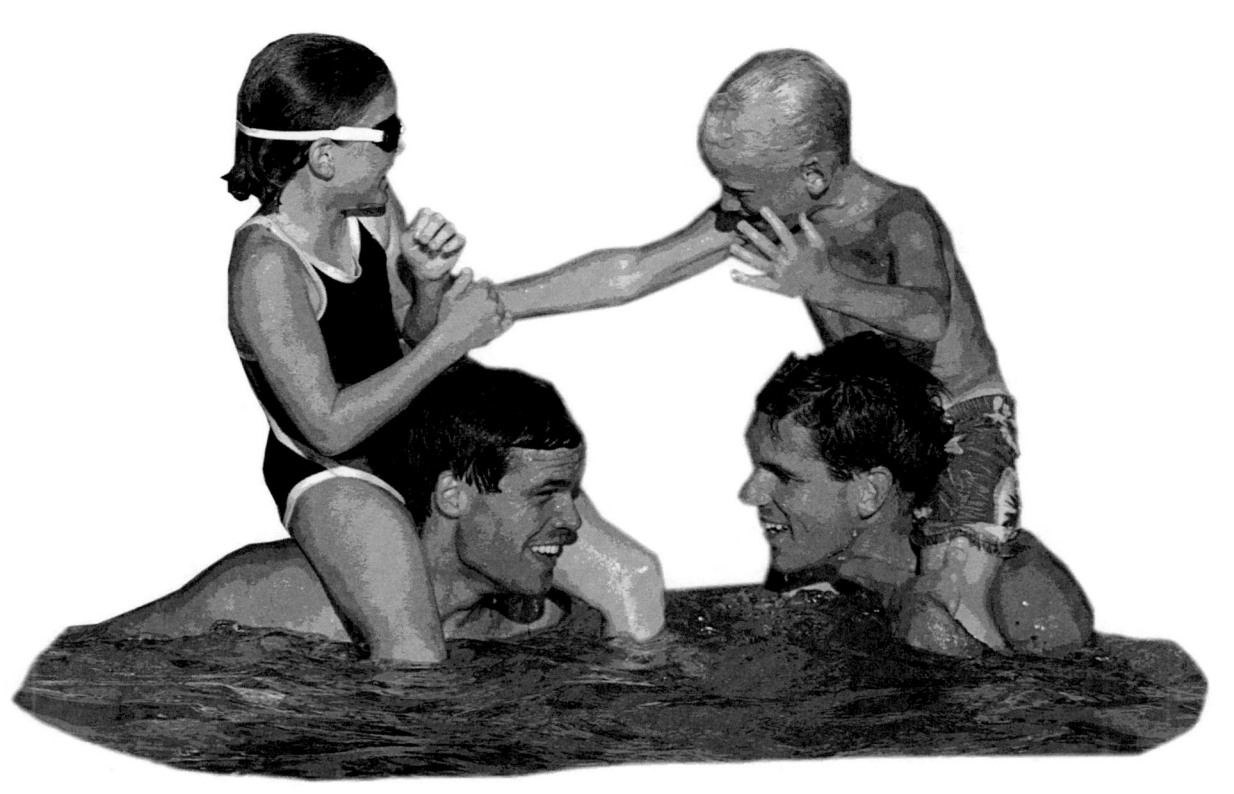

Program Objectives - Week 8

To experience a Playshop with our child/ren.

To assess the value of the Playshop experience.

Facilitator Notes:

Bring any required materials (including name tags).

Arrive early; assist with room set up.

When play areas are set up, gather fathers and children in a large circle.

Welcome the fathers and ask them to introduce their children.

Explain that this is a time for fun and games.

Explain Playshop format and timing (refer to page 58, "Playshop Format"). Mention simple rules for safety (no one hurt) and that no child is to leave the room without an adult.

Act as timekeeper to ensure timely movement between activities. Divide fathers and children into four groups and let the fun begin.

After completing all activities in the Playshop format, end with a large group hug.

---

5 min.   Home Activity

➤ Ask fathers to complete "Observations and Reflections on the Playshop Experience" *(page 75, A Nurturing Father's Journal)*.

Nurturing Relationships I: Fathering Sons/ Fathering Daughters

Program Objectives - Week 9

To discuss the Playshop experience with other group members.

To practice the communication skills of active listening and reflecting.

To explore the unique roles of fathering daughters and fathering sons.

To learn strategies for teaching values to children.

Structured Practice of Active Listening Skills (Using Playshop Observations)

Welcome members and explain that this week's session will begin with a structured activity, the purpose being to simultaneously accomplish the following two goals:
- (1) to give members the opportunity to reflect on and share observations from the Playshop, and
- (2) to experiment with a style of communication called active listening and reflecting.

5 min.   **Part 1 – Communication Skills**

Use the enclosed poster "Communication Skills: Guidelines for Active Listening and Reflecting." Review the guidelines for sending and receiving, and ask the group members to use them in the following discussion.

---

15 min.   **Part 2 – Practice Communication Skills**

Ask members to pair up (choose a partner) and sit comfortably for a private conversation. Ask one member in each pair to be A and the other to be B. A begins the conversation by expressing his observations and feelings about the Playshop. He might discuss what he noticed, what he learned, or how his child/ren did with the experience. B listens actively and attentively and shows A that he truly heard and understood what he was saying by reflecting back what A said.

After five minutes, ask members to stop, reverse roles, and have member B express his thoughts about the Playshop with member A doing the active listening and reflecting. Allow five minutes for this communication , then ask A and B to discuss what they observed and how they felt about this style of communication.

---

15 min.

Part 3 – Focus on the Style of Communication (How We Communicate)

Ask all members to regroup and discuss the activity, which demonstrates a very important lesson about communication.

In terms of relationship building, how we communicate (our style) is more important than what we communicate (the content). Let's look at the how first.

Ask members: "How do you feel after doing this activity?" "How did the style of communication contribute to these feelings?" "What did you experience as speaker/sender and listener/receiver?"

Refer again to the poster "Communication Skills: Guidelines for Active Listening and Reflecting" (this time focusing on re-stating content and linking to feeling). This style of communication will increase openness, foster empathy, and enhance intimacy between father and children. It invites children to be closer and enables them to feel that they're heard and understood. It allows fathers/men to be more receptive to those who are close to them and, as a result, to learn more about what the people with whom they are intimate truly think and feel.

---

10 min.

Part 4 – Focus on the Playshop Experience

Referring to *page 75, A Nurturing Father's Journal,* "Observations and Reflections on the Playshop Experience," ask the group to share brief observations and reflections from the Playshop experience in Session 8.

Communication Skills:
Guidelines for Active Listening and Reflecting
(from *Group Process and Teamwork,* Perlman, 1986)

Nurturing, respectful communication is a *two-way* process involving:

A) Sending - speaking clearly and succinctly, in language easily understood by the child (or other person).

Reminder: We communicate facts as well as feelings, and we communicate with body language and tone of voice, as well as with words.

B) Receiving and Reflecting - listening actively and empathetically by using the following guidelines:

– Listen with a clear and open mind. This is a *receptive* process. Common barriers to active listening are: being preoccupied or distracted; judging and evaluating; anger; formulating responses or arguments; interrupting.

– Listen for content (facts, story line) as well as for feelings.

– Listen deeply for the meaning underlying the words.

– Empathize. Try to put yourself in the child's position or experience.

– Look for nonverbal cues, e.g., body language, facial expression, etc.

The following is particularly effective for listening to children. Once you have actively listened, then simply restate/reflect back what you heard:

Restate the content - paraphrase the facts, story line

&

Link with the feeling - *"And you feel _____."*

Examples:

1. Child says: ***"I hate that teacher for giving me a D. She's dumb."***

   Father responds: ***"Your teacher gave you a D, and you feel angry at her."***

Reminder: Reflecting back feelings is often our "best guess" from what the child is showing us. Allow the child to confirm or correct our impression.

2. Child says: ***"Two days before the dance and he finally asked me. I almost gave up hope!"***

   Father responds: ***"Oh, he finally asked you to the dance, and you feel relieved and happy."***

   Child's inner reaction: ***"Dad, you really understand me."***

This leads to increased openness, trust, and rapport between father and child. It also encourages feelings of self-worth and self-esteem within the child. Active listening and reflecting is a powerful nurturing skill.

15 min.   Break & Snacks

Fathering Daughters/Fathering Sons: Leaving a Legacy

This section provides the opportunity for group members to explore their unique role and influence in fathering sons or daughters. What effect might we have on the development of boys into manhood and girls into womanhood, and on both boys and girls as they learn social skills for mature relationships?

25 min.

Role Modeling and Learning to Relate

Expand on the previous discussion on observations about the Playshop by asking "Did you notice any differences in how we related to sons/boys vs. daughters/girls?" Describe any observations or reflections. Also ask, "Do you feel that a father plays a different role with a son than with a daughter? If so, how would you describe it?" Facilitate a discussion on this theme.

Introduce the following diagram by drawing the following sections on the flip chart or by using the enclosed poster:

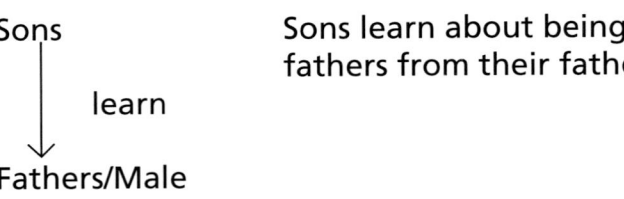

Sons

↓ learn

Fathers/Male

Sons learn about being male and being fathers from their fathers (or father figures).

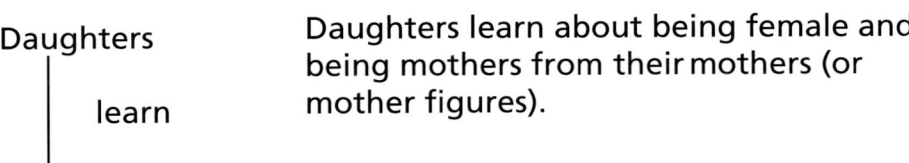

Daughters

↓ learn

Mothers/Female

Daughters learn about being female and being mothers from their mothers (or mother figures).

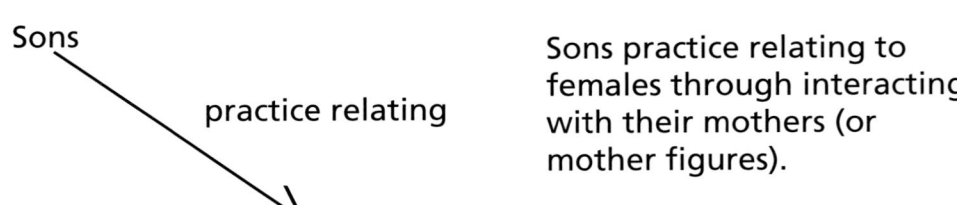

Sons

practice relating

Mothers/Female

Sons practice relating to females through interacting with their mothers (or mother figures).

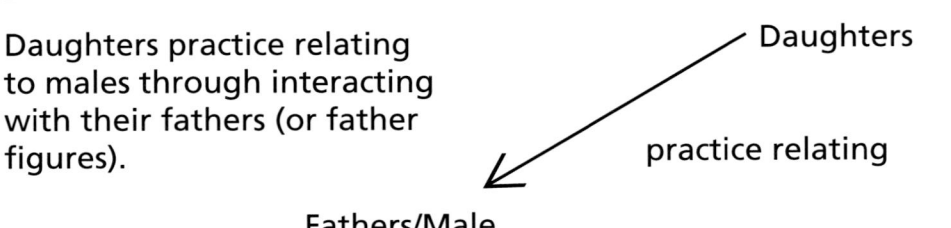

Daughters practice relating to males through interacting with their fathers (or father figures).

Daughters

practice relating

Fathers/Male

The previous sections (with accompanying descriptions) should produce the following completed diagram:

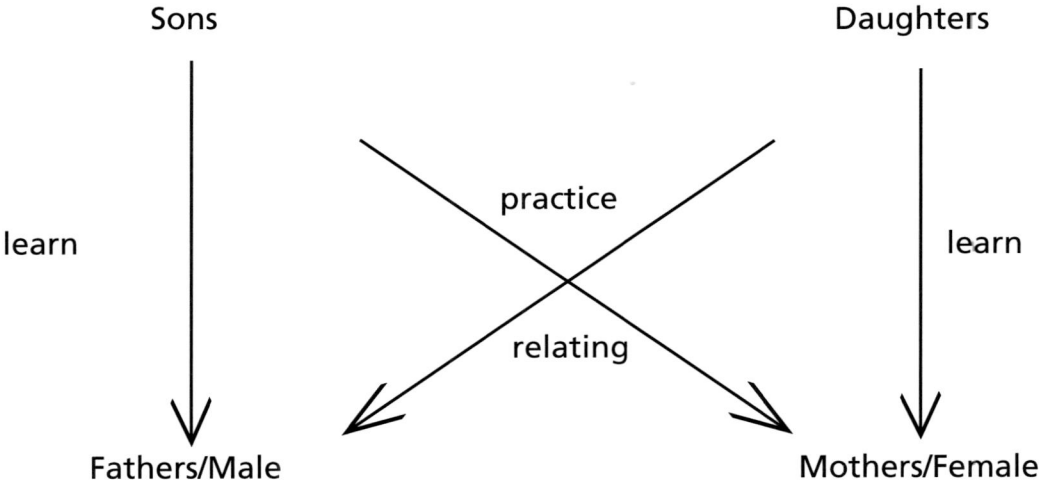

Sons   Daughters

practice

learn   learn

relating

Fathers/Male   Mothers/Female

Role Modeling

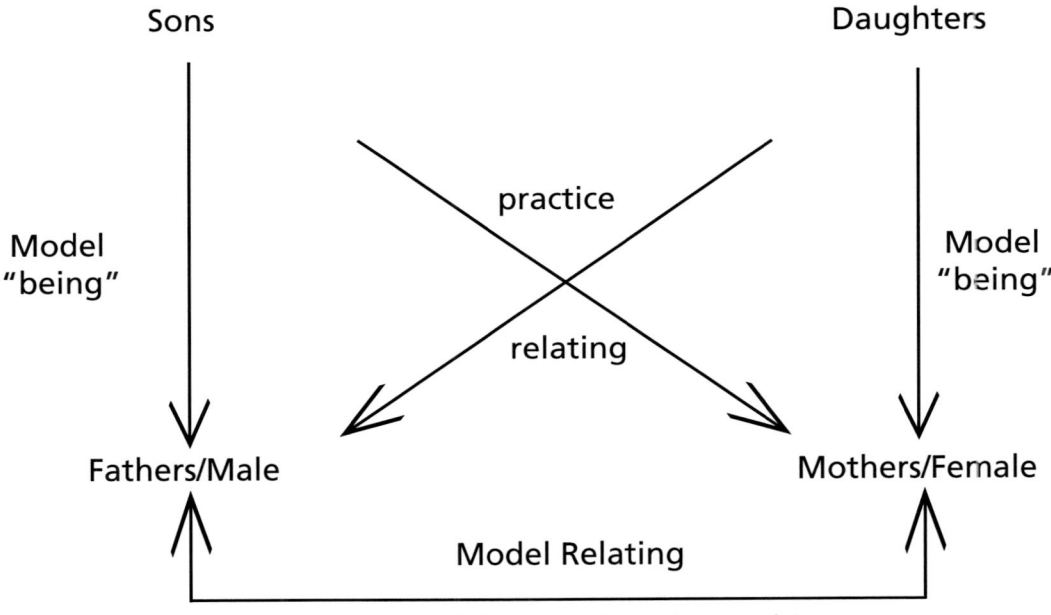

Sons   Daughters

practice

Model   Model
"being"   "being"

relating

Fathers/Male   Mothers/Female

Model Relating

Adult Male-Female Relationship

And, finally, referring to the bottom of the diagram, both daughters and sons learn about adult male-female relationships by observing how fathers/father-figures and mothers/mother-figures relate and interact. Important social skills are learned through the family interactions described in this diagram.

40 min.   Fathering Sons Group/Fathering Daughters Group

Direct members to form two groups, one that will focus on fathering sons and the other that will focus on fathering daughters.

Note: For members who have both sons and daughters, instruct them to choose the group which they feel they would benefit from the most. Reassure them that what both groups discuss will be shared.

Instruct each member in the fathering sons group and fathering daughters group to first spend 10 minutes individually completing the following:

Fathering Sons Group: List what they would like their son to learn about being male/father and how they could teach this to him.

Fathering Daughters Group: List what they would like their daughter to learn about relating to and being treated by men and how they could teach this to her.

Next, instruct each small group to discuss what they concluded from the above activity. Allow 20 minutes for discussion. Ask each group to record its conclusions and to prepare a five-minute presentation of these conclusions. Have each group choose one member to act as its spokesman.

After the small group discussions have been completed, direct members to rejoin into one large group. Ask each spokesman to present the five minute summary of what they discussed and learned from the activity. (Allow for individual values and differences to emerge on issues where group consensus cannot be reached. Everyone does not have to agree because this activity will reveal deeply held values and beliefs. The goal is to bring consciousness and awareness to fathering sons and fathering daughters.)

20 min.   Teaching Values
The previous activity brought forth important values and beliefs concerning being a man, male-female relationships, and basic human values. It is important to respect individual differences in this process and to reflect on what we want to pass on to our sons and daughters, i.e. our legacy. Whatever our personal values are, the following chart presents strategies for teaching values and encouraging value-based behavior in children.

 Write each strategy on a flip chart or use the enclosed poster (Teaching Values) and briefly discuss each category, eliciting specific examples from the group members.

Note: The focus is on how to effectively teach values and value-based behavior. The specific values to teach are left to each individual.

Teaching Values and Encouraging Values-Based Behavior

Role Model. Children learn more from what we do (behavior, actions) than from what we say. Lecturing and moralizing are ineffective tools for teaching values. It is more effective to practice and model the values that we want our children to learn.

Affinity Groups. Starting at an early age, involve a child in groups that reflect the values that are important to you and your family. These groups can be religious, athletic, educational, social, arts, skill-building, etc. Children learn from their psychosocial environment and from having positive peer contact.

Research and provide accurate information on specific topics, e.g., safe driving, drugs and alcohol, race and gender issues, sexual issues, etc. Provide "inform-ation." Ask your children what they think about a subject. (It is often surprising what they know.)

Use active-listening skills to keep communication channels open. Communication is an important link, especially with teens. If we push them away and cut off this channel, we will lose a primary source of influence. Remain open and approachable as a parent.

Rituals. Create rites of passage and celebrations to mark important events or accomplishments. Weave values into these celebrations.

Examples:

Celebrate your son's entering manhood (age 13) with a men's circle of songs, stories, and important messages.

Celebrate your daughter's educational or athletic accomplishments with a special ceremony.

Mark a child's graduation or leaving home with a ceremony that reflects your positive view of their accomplishments and also expresses your best wishes for the future.

Family Rules. Establish rules with your child/ren that reflect family values. (It is important to include older children and teens in formulating rules along with the consequences for breaking them.)

Praise, reward, and pay attention to what your child says or does in order to reflect the values you desire to instill. The more you do this, the more likely your child will be to repeat the behavior that you value.

5 min.   Home Activities

➤ Practice the active listening and reflecting style of communication with your child/ren, spouse, and others. Note the results.

➤ In **A Nurturing Father's Journal,** read and complete "Things To Consider When Fathering Sons" **(page 88-89)** and/or "Things To Consider When Fathering Daughters" **(page 86-87).**

➤ Write a specific conflict or problem that you are currently experiencing with your child/ren and/or partner. You will have the opportunity to work on this at the next group meeting.

End with a group hug.

Notes:

Week 10

Nurturing Relationships II: Teamwork between Father and Spouse/ Co-Parent

Program Objectives - Week 10

To identify the elements of successful teamwork and apply them to co-parenting with spouse/partner.

To learn and practice the skills of negotiation, conflict resolution, and cooperative problem solving.

To practice utilizing a method for dividing household/parenting tasks.

To discuss special issues in fathering, e.g., divorce, step-fathering, single fathering, and grandfathering.

---

15 min.   Home Activities Review
Welcome group members. Ask them what results they noticed when practicing active listening and reflecting. Were there any additional insights related to fathering sons or fathering daughters?

---

30 min.   Elements of Successful Teamwork

Using examples from sports and work, help the group generate specific characteristics/descriptions of how a successful team operates.

Introduce the topic with the following statement: "As men in American society today, we are all familiar with teamwork in sports or work. Quietly reflect for a minute on a specific example of a team that works." (Group members may have been participants or observers in their example.) Ask several members to describe their example. Help identify common themes.

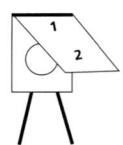

After several examples have been given, ask the group to identify the key elements in successful teamwork. List the responses on a flip chart or blackboard. The list should include:

- Good communication
- Trust
- Reliability
- Clear roles and rules
- Mutual respect
- Support
- Cooperation
- Loyalty (to goals as well as among team members)
- Acknowledging strengths and weaknesses
- Leadership
- Game plan

Ask the group members to apply these elements of successful teamwork to a family, marriage, and co-parenting relationships. Be sure to include and emphasize the value of active listening, negotiation and compromise, cooperative problem solving, accepting differences, sharing power, and honoring commitments.

Negotiation, Conflict Resolution, and Problem Solving

Inform the members that they will now learn and practice specific skills for enhancing successful teamwork between father and spouse (as well as between other family members). Active listening and reflecting (from Week 9) must be practiced here.

15 min.   Negotiation and Conflict Resolution, Part 1

Refer members to **page 100, A Nurturing Father's Journal** and explain that most conflicts and arguments arise from a certain style of thinking and reacting that can be summarized as follows:

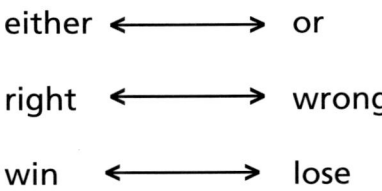

either ⟵⟶ or

right ⟵⟶ wrong

win ⟵⟶ lose

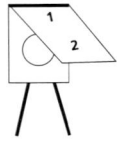

All of these reflect the power-over style. Ask the group members to give examples of conflicts or arguments with a spouse or other person that reflect the above style of thinking and reacting. List the examples on a flip chart or blackboard.

Successful negotiation and conflict resolution require changing thinking and reacting from the above process to the following power-to style:

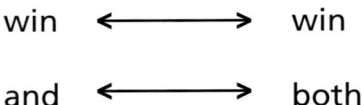

win ⟷ win

and ⟷ both

This is an attempt to incorporate *both* parties' *interests* and *needs* into an outcome that both can accept (or at least live with), instead of trying to defeat the other person. The key consideration in this second type of thinking is being sensitive to the question: "What is *your* interest or need?" Once interests or needs have been identified, then a creative solution can be found that incorporates the interests or needs of both people.

Example #1
The conflict
Person 1:   *"I want to go bowling tonight."*
Person 2:   *"No, I want to invite the Joneses over for dinner."*

Interest/Need
Person 1:   *"I've been sitting all day, and I need to do something active."*
Person 2:   *"I'm interested in being with friends."*

Possible Resolutions
"Might we invite the Joneses to go bowling with us and then get a bite to eat afterward?"

"Maybe we could invite some friends to play volleyball in the backyard, then order food to be delivered."

Example 2:

The conflict

Person 1:   *"I'm tired of always visiting your parents on holidays."*

Person 2:   *"My parents have no other family near them, and you don't seem to care."*

Interest/Need

Person 1:   *"I only have four days off, and I really need to do something fun just for us."*

Person 2:   *" Being close to my parents on holidays is important to me."*

Possible Resolutions

"Maybe we can join my folks for a holiday dinner, then just you and I will drive up to the mountains and go for a hike."

---

15 min.   ## Negotiation and Conflict Resolution, Part 2

Ask group members to pair up and role-play the following:

Begin by choosing one of the conflicts or arguments from the list made earlier.

One member will be father/husband and the other will be the spouse/partner.

Start to role-play the typical conflict/argument.

After a few minutes, one spouse says: "Let's stop for a minute. What is your need/interest here?"

Then practice active listening, negotiation, and cooperative conflict resolution.

After the role-play, ask group members if they experienced the movement from conflict to compromise.

15 min.   ## Break & Snacks

10 min.

Cooperative Problem Solving Model, Part 1

Using the enclosed poster, explain the following steps to address a problem that spouses or parent and child need to resolve together (teamwork in action):

Five-Step Cooperative Problem Solving

1. Define the problem and discuss the facts. Share information and perceptions. Ask what has been tried and how it worked. Where do we want to be/what's the goal?

2. Brainstorm for alternative solutions. This allows a creative and expansive airing of possible solutions. Consider all alternatives. Do not judge, criticize, or evaluate.

3. Prioritize the alternatives and choose a solution. Reality test for strengths, risks, and potential outcomes. Combine ideas and look for positive elements. Listen. Respect each other. Negotiate. Work toward a creative compromise.

4. Put the plan into action. Be clear on expectations, roles, and responsibilities.

5. Evaluation/Feedback. After you have implemented the plan, get back together to discuss how it's working. See if any revisions are needed. (If the plan has failed, go back to step one and work through the steps again to generate another solution.)

(*Group Process and Teamwork,* Perlman, 1986)

Examples of problems:

"We have the house to repair and a vacation planned, but with the doctor bill due we don't have enough money to do both. "

"Jason has gotten his second D in algebra. What are we to do?"

"The company is closing the local office and asking us to relocate, but your job and the kids' school are here."

20 min. Cooperative Problem Solving, Part 2

Ask the group to come up with a typical problem that spouses might encounter. Once the problem has been identified, ask the members to return to their pairs and, referring to the poster, utilize these problem-solving steps *(page 102, A Nurturing Father's Journal)* until a cooperative solution is reached. Be sure the pairs use each step. Then ask each pair to share its solution so that the group can see the range of creative alternatives.

20 min. Special Issues: Divorce, Stepfathering, Single Fathering, Grandfathering, etc.

Facilitate a discussion on successful teamwork issues in the situations of divorce, stepfathering, single fathering, grandfathering, etc. What similarities do these situations have with the strategies discussed in this session? How might you use negotiation, conflict resolution, and cooperative problem solving to address the special issues that accompany these different fathering situations?

10 min. Home Activities

➤ Read the sections on teamwork and co-parenting in *A Nurturing Father's Journal (Week 10).*

➤ Read and complete the activity on dividing household/parenting tasks and responsibilities, *(page 99, A Nurturing Father's Journal)*

End with a group hug.

Notes:

A
Time and
Place
for
Fathering

Program Objectives - Week 11

To assess members' progress and utilize the program tools to assist with problem resolution.

To explore the relationships between time, work, and fathering.

To create a fathering job description that provides the required amount of time for the important fathering duties and activities.

---

60 min.   Assessing progress and troubleshooting.

This time is to be utilized to assess group members' progress and to help the group apply the tools that have been introduced in the program to assist with any problems that a father, child/ren or family member may be experiencing.

Ask group members what is working well at this time, what specific progress or improvement they can notice. Discuss these elements and highlight what has contributed to their success.

Following this discussion, ask members to identify specific problems with which they and/or their family are still struggling. Facilitator should encourage the group to come up with problem solving options, utilizing the tools from this program. The facilitator can help the group identify which Nurturing Father's tools might positively impact the problems presented.

NOTE: This is a good point in the program for the facilitator to identify the members and their child/ren or families who may need additional assistance. The Nurturing Father's Program can help the father identify a need for additional personal or family "work," i.e., individual, couple or family counseling; anger management; drug and alcohol treatment; parenting skills, etc. The facilitator should be prepared to make individual referrals where appropriate.

15 min.   Break & Snacks

15 min.   Time, Work, and Fathering, Part 1

 Write the following three words on a flip chart or blackboard:

TIME   WORK   FATHERING

Facilitate a discussion by asking the group, "What do you feel is the relationship between these three words?" Encourage and allow all comments. Stimulate dialog on what members perceive the issues to be for balancing work and fathering.

 Direct group members to read "A Bridge Between Work and Fathering" using the enclosed poster.

A Bridge Between Work and Fathering:

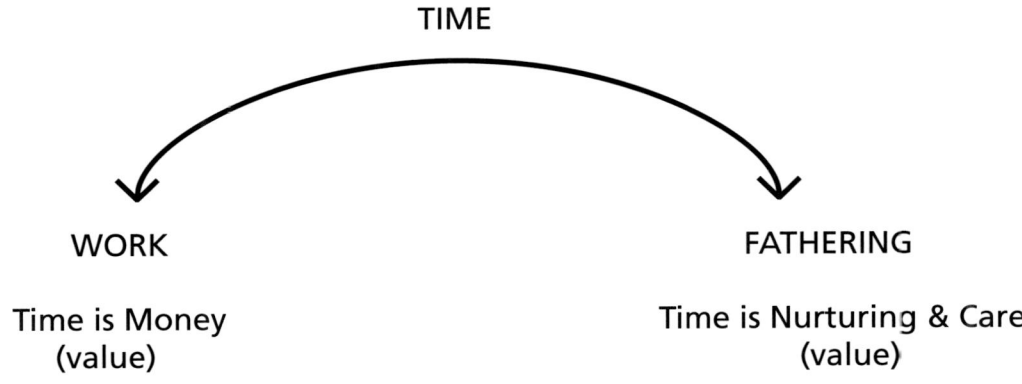

Explain this diagram using the following statements: "Time is of value." "Those things I value deserve my time." "My child/ren are of value. I will give time to my child/ren."
(Allow for group discussion.)

Important Fathering Times

Briefly discuss each of the following:

- Childbirth. Be there with your spouse and new baby.
- Spend a period of time with your spouse, and bonding with your new baby after childbirth.
- Attend parent-teacher conferences and open houses.
- Attend your child's athletic and cultural activities.
- Stay home with a sick child.
- Bring your child to work to show what you do.
- Help with homework and projects.
- Play.
- Share in the mundane tasks, e.g., changing diapers, doing housework, etc.
- Ask members for additional "important fathering times."

End the discussion by asking each member to turn to **page 107, *A Nurturing Father's Journal*** and to write the name(s) of their child(ren) in the blank spaces as directed in "Commitment." Then ask for silence, as each group member quietly reads "Commitment" to himself.

---

15 min. **Father's Duties and Responsibilities, Part 2**

Organize the group members into three small groups, according to age range of their children (if any member's children span several ranges, suggest that they choose the group with which they would feel most comfortable).

Group 1: children from newborn to 5.

Group 2: children from 6-12.

Group 3: children 13 and older.

Provide each group a piece of flip chart paper and a marker. Direct the members to brainstorm a list of all the duties, responsibilities, and activities, etc., that are required for the parent of children in that age range. Request that the groups limit their discussion and work toward creating a complete list.

Once the lists have been compiled, collect the flip chart lists and tape them around the room so that they are visible to all the members. Then, on the bottom of each list of fathering duties, add, "And other duties as required."

---

20 min. **My Fathering Job Description, Part 3**

Ask the group members to work individually, referencing the lists that are posted around the room, and complete "My Fathering Job Description" *(page 111, A Nurturing Father's Journal).*

For each duty, responsibility, or activity that appears on their list, assign a realistic amount of time (either per day or per week) that the duty/responsibility/activity requires in order to do the job right. Remind the members to be realistic and fair, and that they will evaluate their job performance according to this job description.

Remind the group when 10 minutes has elapsed so that the members will have enough time to complete the job description. Any members who feel they need more time to complete this activity should be instructed to finish it as a home activity.

---

20 min. **Discuss "Additional Consideration Regarding Work and Fathering," Part 4**

Work can have a profound influence on fathering, beyond the obvious aspect of the availability of time. An over-involvement with work can result in the classic absentee father, who has little time for family or fathering. Work can also have more subtle, yet extremely important, influences on fathering. Ask for a show of hands as you read each of the following to indicate if group members feel it applies to them:

- Lack of physical energy and availability: "Would like to, but I'm just too tired."

- Lack of emotional energy and availability. The father who is physically present but emotionally absent.

- Increased frustration and a short temper, often expressed by yelling and hitting: "One more thing and I'll . . ."

- Dictatorial style/high control needs: "Why can't I run my family like I run my shop (organization, business, etc.)?"

- Having training sufficient for the challenges at work but little or no training to face the challenges at home: "Work problems I can fix. Home/kids problems are much tougher."

- Little control or autonomy at work; need to feel in control at home: "I'm tired of being told what to do. It's time for me to tell someone else what to do."

Be conscious of how work can affect the quality of fathering.

---

5 min.   **Home Activities**

➤ Read "Commitment" *(page 107, A Nurturing Father's Journal)* and "My Fathering Job Description" *(page 111, A Nurturing Father's Journal)*. Refer to these journal pages often during the coming week as you balance work, time, and fathering.

➤ Complete the activity entitled "The Joys of Fathering" *(page 112, A Nurturing Father's Journal)*.

NOTE: Remind group members that it is very important to set aside time to do the home activities.

End with a group hug.

Healing the Father Wound

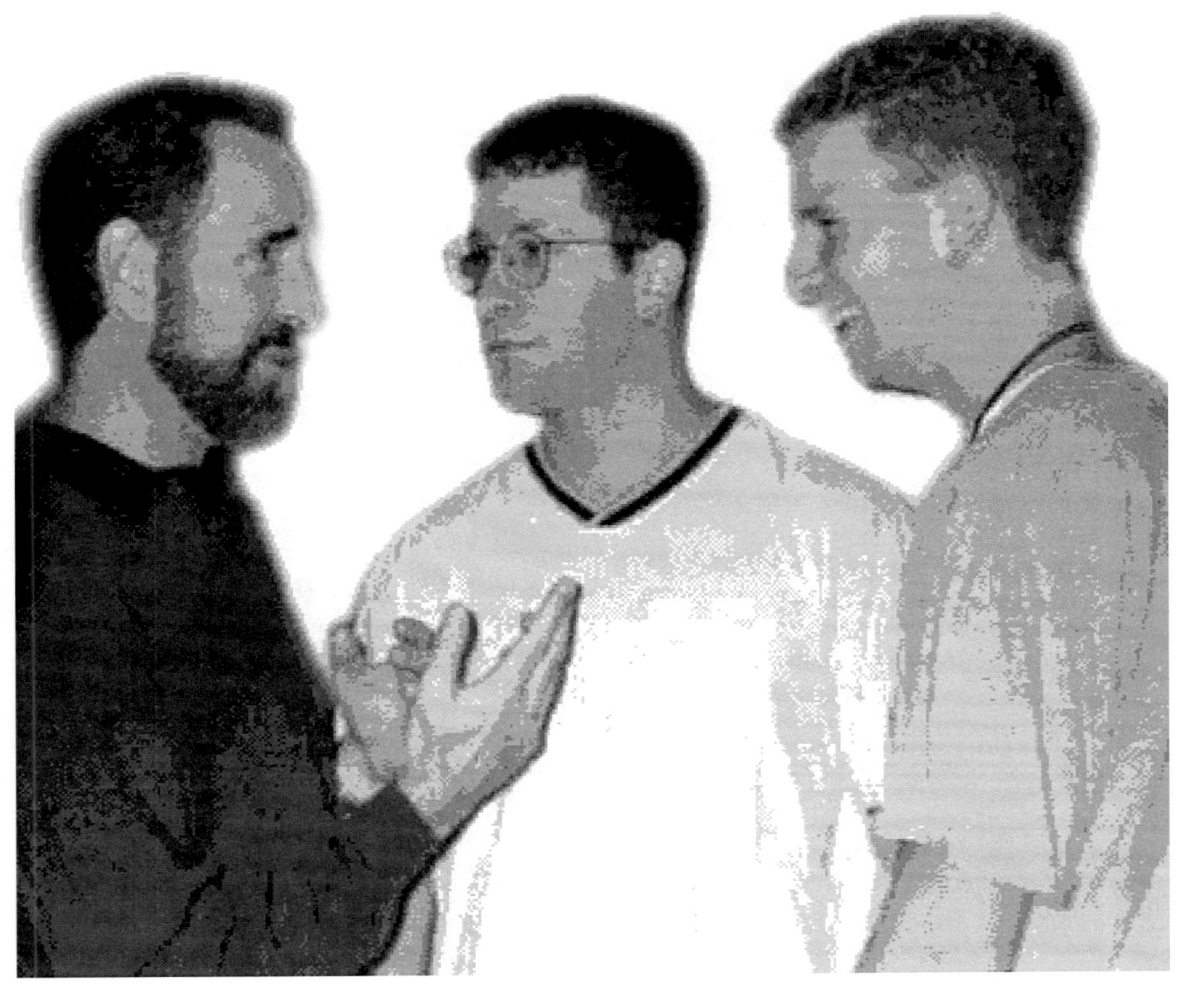

Program Objectives - Week 12

To reflect upon the special joys of fathering.

To reflect upon the things we would have liked
  to have heard from our father.

To experience receiving nurturing fathering
  messages.

To choose the messages we would like our
  child/ren to hear from us.

---

20 min.   Home Activities Review

Direct the group members to turn to the home activity "Joys of
Fathering" *(page 112, A Nurturing Father's Journal).* Ask them
to read and reflect upon what they wrote for this activity, then
to choose a few special joys to share with the group. Facilitate
a free-form sharing of the most memorable moments and
delights of fathering.

Healing the Father Wound

Since none of us had all of our childhood needs met by our father,
we, as adults, often carry a "wound." It is that hurt or unhealed
part of us that suffers from the limitations, imperfections, absence,
or excesses of our father. Some men received little or no love from
their father. Others received little or no time, attention, or nurturing. Still others experienced anger, criticism, or possibly even
abuse. And some experienced a cold distance or inability to reach
their father. In all cases, the limitations/imperfections of our father
have left us with longings . . . longings for those things we truly
needed but did not get.

Some men, as adults, are able to achieve the type of relationship
with their father that they wished for as a child. This enables them
to get their needs met and to have the relationship healed. As a
result, they no longer carry the father wound. For most men,
however, the wound persists unhealed, and this can present a
barrier to being the nurturing father that they would like to be.

The experiences of this program have presented many opportunities for encouraging the group members to identify aspects of their father wound and share healing experiences with other men/fathers. This frees them to be the nurturing father that each person is capable of being.

The activities that follow should be a powerful opportunity to deepen the healing and to promote the emergence of nurturing fathering. It is also an experience where men can nurture and receive nurturing from other men.

---

15 min.   **The Things I Needed To Hear**

Explain the father wound, using the above information. Allow for any discussion that the group members need but limit the discussion.

Direct each member to complete "The Things I Needed To Hear" *(page 117, A Nurturing Father's Journal).* Ask the members to work individually and quietly, encouraging them to reach deeply into themselves to access their true thoughts and feelings.

After 10-15 minutes, direct the members to review what they have written and either (1) circle the statement that is the one they would have loved to have heard the most, or (2) construct that most nurturing statement.

---

40 min.   **The Nurturing Father's Circle**

Each group member is to utilize his "most nurturing statement" from the prior activity in the following activity by saying it to others.

Separate the group into two halves (you can count off 1,2,1,2,1,2, etc.)

Place chairs for half the group in a close circle and direct the 1's to sit silently in these chairs.

Direct each 2 to stand behind a 1, place his hands on the person's shoulders, and lean over and say his own "most nurturing statement" to this group member exactly as he would have liked to have heard it himself, e.g., "You are perfect, exactly as you are," "I love you," "I am so glad that you are my son." Those who are seated should not respond or speak, only listen and take in what is being said. The 2's should wait a moment, then say the message a second time.

Then each of the 2's (standing) should move to the right and repeat his statement twice to the next person. Pause for a moment; then move on. Continue until the circle is complete, and each 2 is standing behind the 1 where he started.

Next, all 1's stand and the 2's take the seats. Repeat the process, with each 2 receiving a most nurturing message from each 1. Be sure the message is said twice to each seated person.

Afterward, allow group to "process" their feelings and thoughts (prior to the break). First, give members a few minutes to reflect or to write. Then, discuss the experience. Be sure to encourage underlying feelings to be expressed.

20 min.   Break & Snacks

Facilitator: During break and snacks this week, hand out the The Nurturing Father's Program Evaluation and ask members to complete the form and return it by the end of the break.

30 min.   The Things I Need To Say

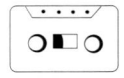

Direct members to complete "The Things I Need to Say" **(page 118, A Nurturing Father's Journal).** Ask members to work separately and quietly. Allow 15 minutes for this part.

When all members have completed the above exercise, ask them to choose a partner. The two should then discuss their statements from "The Things I Need to Say." Encourage each member to support his partner in his commitment to say his most nurturing messages to his child/ren. (Advise the group when 10 minutes have elapsed so that all the members will have time to share.) Allow 15 minutes for this discussion.

15 min.   Nurturing Father Visualization

Direct all members to regroup and to sit comfortably and quietly. The following visualization should be read slowly and softly.

Use enclosed audio tape (Side A) for a narrative presentation of this visualization or read aloud using audio tape (Side B) for musical background to accompany your reading.

"We are about to take a relaxing and nurturing journey together. It is perfectly safe, so let yourself relax and let go. First, take a deep breath . . . and exhale. Now, another deep breath . . . and let it out. And one more deep breath . . . As you exhale, all stress and tension flows out. Now we will breathe gently together. Feel a warmth at the soles of your feet. As you breathe in, this warmth becomes a gentle, golden glowing light. With your next breath, the golden glow surrounds your feet and legs. It is a soft and safe glowing light. Breathe in, and the glow spreads up to your genitals and waist. Any sexual tension disappears. Breathe in, and the glow spreads up through your stomach and chest. You experience a loving, peaceful feeling.

Breathe the golden light up into your shoulders and arms. All worries and fears become dissolved. And breathe the golden light up your neck and feel it surround your head. You feel warm, safe, and alive. (pause)

Now, breathing comfortably, you notice the golden light forms a path that extends before you. As you look up the path, a source of golden glow can be seen at the end. It calls you, and you want to go to it. So you begin walking along the golden path, your body still radiating the gentle golden light. You feel happy and excited. As you walk along the path, the golden glow at the end becomes larger and larger, almost like a sun. But it cannot burn or hurt you. As you approach it, you can see a face in the glowing light. It is gentle, warm, and smiling, yet amazingly powerful. Take a moment to see and feel this presence. (pause)

Then you hear a voice saying, "Come a step closer. I have something to tell you." You take a step closer, putting your ear next to the mouth of this sun-like face. Listen, it will tell you exactly what you need to hear from this nurturing figure. (pause)

As you hear the message, you also feel lovingly held and hugged, peaceful and safe, with glowing golden light all around you. (pause)

Now, take a step back. Look at the smiling, glowing sun-face and say, "Thank you." And as you turn and start back down the golden path, you notice that the gentle golden glow still surrounds your body. That light is always with you. It is your power to nurture yourself and others. (pause)

Now, take a deep breath. Feel the chair under you, and the floor beneath your feet. And gently open your eyes and return to this room and all of us here."

Take a few minutes to allow the members to share anything they feel they want to.

10 Min. Home Activities and Preparations for Graduation

Remind the group that next week is the last meeting. It will be a special graduation celebration to which child/ren and spouse/ partner are invited.

Explain the following format for the two hour Graduation Ceremony:

First Hour - Children and Family Members Present
- Welcome and Introductions.
- Each group member reads his "Commitment To My Family: The Father I Choose To Be" and receives his graduation certificate.
- Food and Social Time (After social time, children and family members leave.)

Second Hour - For Group Members (Fathers) Only
  Group members share group and personal feedback (closure).

➤ Invite your child/ren and spouse/partner, or other family members, to join you for the last meeting of the *Nurturing Father's Program.*

➤ Complete "Commitment To My Family: The Father I Choose To Be" *(page 124, A Nurturing Father's Journal).* Be sure all members bring this with them next week to read to their child/ren and other family members.

➤ Plan to bring special food, snacks and drinks to add to the celebration.

End with a group hug.

Facilitator Reminder: Prepare a certificate for every group member who completed the program. Also bring name tags and some special food or treat to add to next week's celebration (e.g., a "Nurturing Fathers Congratulations" cake). If you desire, decorations will add a celebratory touch. An on-site child care arrangement may be needed for some of the children during the second hour of the graduation activities.

Week 13

Graduation Ceremony and Closing Activity

Program Objectives - Week 13

To review the goals and purpose of the Nurturing Father's Program.

To have each group member read his commitment to his family.

To celebrate and experience closure by giving and receiving feedback with other group members.

Facilitator Preparations: Arrive early!

Bring name tags for each person.

Bring the program certificates to be distributed during the closing ceremony.

Set up tables for the food and drinks.

Arrange chairs in a large circle.

Decorate (if you planned to do this).

Create an atmosphere of celebration.

Welcome each father and his family as they arrive.

---

15 min.   Opening Activity: Welcome and Introductions

Welcome everyone and express appreciation for their being here. Ask each father to introduce himself and his family members.

Briefly state the purpose and goals of *The Nurturing Father's Program* and anything else you would like to add as a welcoming introduction.

45 min.   **Graduation Ceremony**

Announce, "Each group member has prepared a statement of commitment to read to his family, and it's called "The Father I Choose To Be."

Ask one father to volunteer to read his statement. (Suggest that the father face his family while reading.) After he has finished, present him with his certificate and applaud him. Then ask his family members if they would like to say anything before moving on to the next group member. Continue this process until every group member and his family have had a chance to speak.

After all members have read their commitment statements, ask for any additional comments before food and social time.

Have a large family circle group hug and thank children and familymembers for being here.

15 min.   **Break & Snack**

60 min.   **Group and Individual Feedback**

After children and family members have left, call the group members back together.

Ask each group member to make a brief statement about the group, the program, and what this experience has meant to him.

As each group member completes his statement, ask other members to share a few thoughts and feelings with that member. Topics could include: what they like about him; respect about him; changes they've observed in him. (Write these three options on a flip chart.)

Continue this process until each group member has had the opportunity to give and receive feedback.

Finally, Facilitator should say whatever he feels is appropriate for closing, being sure to mention the following:

Remind group members that there is a Slam Book page in the back of their *Nurturing Father's Journal* for autographs, phone numbers, and messages.

Encourage the members to keep in touch, possibly even meet together as a support group.

Encourage members to sign up for a Nurturing Program for Parents and Children in which the entire family participates. (Hand out a flier for the next scheduled program.) Hand out fliers for upcoming parenting programs.

Thank group members for their participation in the program.

End with a group hug!

ORDER FORM

Please select the item, noting the quantity and amount, then phone, fax or mail your order to us.
Indicate choice of materials written in English or Spanish in quantity column.

Qty. Eng	Qty. Spn	Description	Item Code	Price	Amount
		Nurturing Father's Program **Starter Kit - Special Price** contains 10 Journals/Workbooks, 1 Facilitator Manual, 1 Posters/PowerPoint CD, 1 Forms CD, 1 Visualizations CD	NFP Starter	$379	
		Complete Nurturing Father's Program (2 manuals, 20 journals and all materials)	NFP	$650	
		(FOR RE-ORDERS ONLY) **Nurturing Father's Journal (bound)**	JOU	$15	
		Facilitator Manual	FAC	$89	
		Confidentiality Agreements **Program Evaluation Forms** } ON CD FOR COPYING **Certificates of Achievement**	CER	$59	
		Posters (Set of 11)	POS	$99	
		Power Point CD (expanded poster set)	POS-CD	$99	
		Visualizations/Audio CD	VIS	$29	
				Subtotal	
				FL only, 7% sales tax	
				Shipping & Handling	
				TOTAL	

Shipping & Handling:
Continental U.S.
Orders $15 and under, add $5
Orders $15 - $100, add $15
Orders over $100, add 10%

Foreign Orders:
Actual Shipping Cost plus 10% Handling.

Special Shipping Requests:
Costs of extra shipping charges (2nd Day Air, etc.) will be added to invoice.

Hawaii, Alaska, Canada:
For orders under $100, add $20
For orders over $100, add 20%

Please check method of payment:
(All orders must be prepaid.)

☐ Check or money order enclosed
(Payable to Center for Growth & Development, Inc.)

Charge my ☐ Visa   ☐ MasterCard

Account # _____ Exp. Date: _____

Sec. Code _____

Signature _____ Date: _____

All prices in U.S. currency. Prices subject to change without notice.
All orders must include shipping.

Ship to:
This is a   ☐ Business ☐ Residential Address
(Unless otherwise specified, all orders are shipped via UPS to street addresses - no PO boxes please.)

Name _____

Agency _____

Address _____

City/State/ZIP _____

Daytime Phone _____

E-mail Address _____

For Information About Programs or Training Workshops, call toll-free 1-888-390-1119 or visit our website at www.nurturingfathers.com

"The supreme test of any civilization is whether or not it can teach men to become good fathers."
— Margaret Mead

The Nurturing Father's Program
By Mark Perlman, MA

*A 13-Week Group-based Curriculum
for Developing Attitudes and Skills for Male Nurturance*

NEW!

Starter Kit

No special training required. Just open the Starter Kit and get started.
(Facilitator Training is available upon request.) Over 15 Years of PROVEN Success.
continuous evidence from pre and post data; feedback from fathers (and mothers);
feedback from facilitators. To learn more, check us out on
www.nurturingfathers.com • www.facebook.com/nurturingfathers • www.youtube.com/nurturingfathers

Program materials include:

- A comprehensive Facilitator Manual with step-by-step instructions for guiding group members toward achieving the specific learning objectives developed for each two and one half hour weekly meeting.

- A Nurturing Father's Journal, the interactive workbook containing weekly home activities for each group member to complete in order to enhance his knowledge and growth.

- A set of posters to be used as teaching aids and to make facilitation easier.

- An audio CD with prerecorded, guided visualization activities.

- Confidentiality Agreements, Program Evaluation forms, Certificates of Achievement, CD for printing forms

Program activities address:

- The Roots of Fathering
- Nurturing Our Children and Ourselves
- Fathering Sons/Fathering Daughters
- Discipline
- Without Violence
- Play
- Managing Anger/Resolving Conflict
- Teamwork with Spouse/Partner
- Communication/Problem Solving
- Balancing Work and Fathering
- Cultural Influences
- Dealing with Feelings
- The Father I Choose To Be

From Men Who Have Completed This Program:

"... a fantastic journey/education into learning healthy fathering." Married father of a 16-month old

"...made me realize that by nurturing my children, I grow myself." Married father of two teenage children

"I survived my divorce, stayed focused on my children, and took care of myself because of this program..." Single father of two children

"...will most definitely make fathers out of men." Divorced father of 38- and 36-year olds, grandfather of 17-, 12-, 10-, 4-, and 2-year olds

"Forget all the books, the audio tapes, and what your family and relatives have said and take this course." Married father of 6- and 9-year olds

"...will do more for my children and my relationship with them than anything else I could imagine." Stepfather of 4-, 8-, and 10-year olds

See reverse side for ordering information